Child Development from Birth to Eight

A Practical Focus

Published by the National Children's Bureau
8 Wakley Street
London
EC1V 7QE
Tel: +44(0)20 7843 6000

Registered Charity No. 258825

© National Children's Bureau 1993

Reprinted 1994, 1999, 2004, 2006

ISBN:1 904787 282

Printed by CPI Bath

As an umbrella body for the children's sector in England and
Northern Ireland, we provide essential information on policy,
research and best practice for our members and other partners.

NCB promotes the voices, interests and well-being of all children
and young people across every aspect of their lives.

Contents

All photographs in this book are posed by models.

Cover photograph by John Birdsall.

Acknowledgements

This booklet was developed from a resource on child development included in *Ensuring Standards in the Care of Young Children* – a training pack for officers registering or inspecting day care under the Children Act 1989 published by the National Children's Bureau. The original material benefited from the suggestions given by members of the group who worked on that publication.

I am grateful to the following people who gave constructive suggestions for re-drafting the material as a separate publication for a wider potential readership:

Babette Brown, Early Years Trainers Anti-Racist Network
Margaret Buttigieg, Director, Health Visitors' Association
Mary Jane Drummond, Cambridge Institute of Education
Janet Evans, Head, Ditton Fields Nursery School, Cambridge
Sheila Gatiss, Preschool Playgroups Association
Sue Griffin, National Childminding Association
Margaret Hanney, Head, Early Childhood Unit (Wales)
Jane Lane, Education Officer, Commission for Racial Equality
Carol Joseph, Black Child Care Network
Gillian Pugh, Director, Early Childhood Unit
Dorothy Rouse, Development Officer, Early Childhood Unit
Maureen Smith, National Nursery Examination Board
Jill Wheeler, Probation Officer, London.
John Wheeler, Assessment and Care Plan Manager, Westminster Social Services
Sheila Wolfendale, Department of Psychology, University of East London

I have written the material with a full commitment to the values that underpin all the work of the Early Childhood Unit. I take responsibility, of course, for the particular way of expressing views about children and organising the material on development.

Jennie Lindon
March 1993

Foreword

One of the Bureau's central purposes has always been to raise awareness of the needs and rights of children, and we are therefore delighted that Jennie Lindon has been able to expand some earlier work that she did for the Early Childhood Unit into this accessible and authoritative book on child development from birth to eight years. Raising awareness is important, but it is not sufficient in itself: we don't only need to know how children learn and develop, but also how to ensure that adults understand that learning and development, and know how they can support it.

In their first eight years children are growing and developing at a breath-taking rate. But whilst all children pass through similar stages in their development, each child is unique. And just as children will always vary as individuals, so will the way in which families bring up their children be different. In responding to children and their families, we may recognise common patterns, but we must be wary of generalisations. As the book points out, there are many different ways to raise healthy children.

Large numbers of people come into contact with young children during the course of their daily lives. Some work directly with them – teachers, health visitors, playgroup leaders, childminders, nursery workers, play workers; others are with children less frequently but need to understand how they grow and develop and how to respond appropriately to them – social workers, police officers, registration and inspection officers looking at the quality and care offered by nurseries. And of course parents, who know their children better than anyone, but sometimes want to look at them within a broader context.

We hope that this short book will make an important contribution to all adults' understanding and enjoyment of children. I would like to thank the Department of Health and Halifax Building Society for their kind contributions towards the production of this book.

Gillian Pugh
Early Childhood Unit
National Children's Bureau
July 1993

The author

Jennie Lindon is a psychologist and works as an independent consultant and trainer. She has written numerous articles and books on children and their families – most recently – **Caring for the Under-8s – working to achieve good practice** published by Macmillan and **Your Child from 5-11** published by Hodder and Stoughton.

Introduction

What are the aims of this book?

The main aims are to provide:

- some pointers on how to make sense of child development, including the reasons why it is important to be careful in how you come to conclusions;
- a description of what children learn in the years from birth to eight and how they change in the different aspects to their development;
- some explanation of how children learn and, therefore, how adults can best help children as they develop and change.

Who might use the book?

It has been written for people who need practical information on the under eights and their development. You could find the contents very useful if:

- in your job you need to have an accurate picture of child development but you do not work exclusively with children.

    For instance, you might be a police officer or a social worker working mainly with adults;
- the children you encounter through your job are in trouble for some reason, or you think it very likely that their pattern of development or behaviour may be unusual.

    You might be in a specialised role such as working within a child protection team. You want a rounded knowledge of children in general, in order to approach the concerns you have about individual children, their parents or carers;
- you are an early years worker in contact with children and their families on a daily basis.

    You might be a nursery officer, a teacher or a worker in a holiday club. You have a good basis of knowledge about children. However, you need to remind yourself and to keep up to date with fresh ways of looking at the under eights, their development and how best to work with them;

- you are caring for babies and children in the home – as a parent, childminder or a nanny.

   The booklet could help you to make sense of the development of the individual children you know well and to extend your understanding of how best to spend your time with them.
- you are advising or training or inspecting any of the other potential groups of readers.

A book of this length will not, of course, tell you **everything** you may wish to know. It will give a firm basis for identifying what else you might need to find out. The suggestions for further reading at the end of the book will give you some possible directions to follow.

Reading and using this book

You could, if you wish, read this book through in one sitting. You could just as usefully read it in several sittings. It is very likely that you will go back over the sections as your interest leads.

   Anyone's knowledge of child development builds up gradually and needs refreshing at regular intervals. However experienced you may be, you should always be ready to review your knowledge and the perspectives that you bring to bear on your contact with under eights and their families.

Why under eights?

Until recent years British publications on practical aspects to child development have divided up childhood into the under and over fives.

   There is no basis in child development for making the break at five years. The reason has been that, in Britain, children have to start school, or an accepted alternative form of education, in the term of their fifth birthday. Starting full time school is an important event in the lives of young children. However, other countries in the world start their children at six or seven years of age.

   The years from the fifth to the eighth birthday are a continuation of the development of those earlier years. Of course, eight-year-olds are not suddenly mini-adults but their development has taken many of them to the point where they can learn more independently. They relate to adults and other children in a different way.

Part one: Making sense of child development

Many people who work with the under eights and their families want some way to make sense of what an individual child can manage and how he or she has changed in recent months or over the years. The following kind of questions are asked:

'It looks to me as if this child is doing really well for her age. Am I right?'

'I'm surprised by what this child does (or says), but should I be worried?'

'I think that this parent (or worker) doesn't offer very suitable activities for the children. How can I support what I'm suggesting?'

This part to the book guides you to the points you should bear in mind when making sense of children's development. Part two takes a look at children as a whole. Part three describes how children change from birth to eight years in the different aspects to their whole development. In each area of development there are practical suggestions on how any adult can best help children.

Is there such a thing as normal development?

If by 'normal development' you mean an exact pattern that all children follow, worldwide, at ages defined in years and months, the answer has to be 'No'.

If you are asking for a description of the kind of stages that babies and children pass through and an approximate age range when the development is happening, then the reply can be a cautious 'Yes'. However, it is probably less confusing to talk of shared stages rather than normal development.

The danger of unchecked assumptions

Professionals working with and for children have become very wary of using the phrase 'normal development'. This caution has grown with the awareness that unjustifiable assumptions have sometimes been part of this outlook in the past. Two examples follow of relatively common, inaccurate assumptions:

Example one
Writers and early years workers, who are themselves only fluent in one language, may believe that it is natural for all children to learn to speak a single language, until taught a foreign language in school.

This assumption has often led to the conviction that bilingual children must, of necessity, have problems. In fact, learning more than one language within early childhood is part of normal language development for many children around the world.

Example two
Some books describe children's physical needs or give symptoms of common illnesses as if all children were White.

Symptomatic rashes will show up differently depending on the colour of a child's skin. Black children's skin and hair requires a different kind of care to that of White children. Both are equally normal, just different.

Don't lose individual children in the averages

As much as children share similar stages in development, you still have to look at any individual child as a unique person. Anyone concerned for children's well being is forever balancing up two related ways of looking at an individual child:

- How is this child progressing if she or he is compared with other children of a similar age?
- How has this child changed over the last few months or the last year – that is, compared with herself or himself in the past?

Whenever you are considering children's development or their behaviour, for whatever reason, you need to gather together a full picture of an individual child. It will be risky to focus on just one side of development or single events, however striking these may appear at first sight.

Children with disabilities

Some children will vary significantly in the pace of their development if you are comparing them with other children of a similar age.

For example, a child with Down's Syndrome may follow many of the developmental steps described in part three but may spend longer than average at each stage. Children with a severely disabling physical condition may be very restricted in what will ever be possible in physical development, especially if access to suitable equipment is limited.

Physical or mental disabilities will make a difference to a child's pattern of development. Even children who share the same disability will vary in their development, depending on the severity and the extent of the condition as it affects them and the opportunities that are offered to them.

The two ways of looking at a child's development are important for all children, but can be especially relevant when you are working with children with disabilities. Parents and workers need an accurate assessment of how a disability appears to be affecting a child's development, compared with children of a similar age but who do not experience this disability. Yet an individual child's progress can also be celebrated in terms of what she or he has learned, compared with a few weeks or months earlier.

> Children's special needs will be determined by the disability or continuing health condition that they experience. However, their special needs should be seen as additional and complementary to all the needs that they share with other children — because they are first and foremost children.

Children who are gifted

The term 'special needs' also refers to children whose development is significantly advanced for their age.

Children who are gifted intellectually or who have a prodigious talent may still have much in common with children of a similar age. They will need appropriate challenge to develop their talent or skill and their special needs can be met without making their childhood a joyless experience. Newsworthy stories have tended to focus on those children and their families in which all other childhood pursuits have been apparently lost in the drive for excellence in only one area of endeavour.

There are different ways to raise healthy children

Different children within the same family

Children will always vary as individuals. Such differences will originate from some combination of the effects of nature (the tendencies that a child has inherited through the genes) and nurture (the impact of all the child's experiences).

Even brothers and sisters raised in apparently the same way in the same family can be very different one from another. They vary in their interests,

Adrian Rowland

how they form friendships and how they handle the usual challenges of childhood.

Of course, even in the same family, children are not treated exactly the same. They should be treated fairly but it is probably impossible to treat them in exactly the same way. From the earliest days, babies behave slightly differently. This variation in turn has an impact on how adults behave towards the baby – let alone that family circumstances or stresses may be quite different around the birth of different children.

Of course, some parents deliberately vary their behaviour towards children. For example, many families, from diverse cultural traditions, treat sons and daughters differently.

Cultural tradition and child rearing

How any family raises their children will influence to a certain extent how a child develops. Family style will create some opportunities for children, whilst removing or restricting others.

Human beings are not born knowing how to care for babies and children. Girls and boys learn the kind of behaviour that is expected of them within their own family and the wider community.

Children's pattern of development will be influenced by their family's beliefs about child rearing. Family practice will be a unique mix of personal style and of cultural traditions passed between the generations. Some practices are shaped by religious beliefs, or other strongly held views on right and wrong.

> Traditions change between generations within the same social or cultural group. Such changes can remind everyone that what children are able to achieve is shaped, at least in part, by adults' expectations of them.
>
> If you compare current English childcare books with those popular in the 1950s, you will find conflicting advice as well as consistent themes.
>
> For example, you will find equally confident, differing predictions of when children should be reliably toilet trained or whether you should feed babies on demand or to a strict time schedule.

Britain as a multicultural society

For centuries, Britain has been a country with a blend of diverse cultures and the impact of different languages – both in the development of English as a living language and distinct languages like Welsh and Gaelic.

Within the twentieth century, society has developed to encompass even greater diversity of culture, ethnicity, religion and language. Britain is a multicultural society, although the particular mix within a local population varies from place to place. Consequently, everyone involved with children and their families should be open to learning about different cultural traditions in care of babies, diet and how children are expected to behave.

A responsible approach to children and families

Be very wary of generalisations

Without a broad base of knowledge, you may assume that a few known individuals are typical of how any adult in a particular culture, part of the country or even age group will behave towards children.

You should be wary of making any generalisation from an individual to a group or from beliefs you hold about a social or ethnic group to predictions about one individual. This proper caution should hold you back from generalisations about 'parents' in general, or 'teenage mothers' as much as from generalising about 'African families' or 'Muslims'.

John Birdsall

Ask yourself would you be happy to be taken as a typical example of your social or ethnic group — even if the generalisation were complimentary?

If you would want to say, 'It all depends...' then why are you assuming that groups (social, cultural, religious) to which you do not belong should be less varied than your own sources of identity?

Should you accept any tradition?

Responsible adults need to understand traditions different from their own and to respect them. This does not mean that you would accept a practice that was abusive of children. It would not matter how many years of tradition lay behind such behaviour.

It would be very important that you could support your views by reference to children's physical or emotional well being. Without such support, other people could conclude, perhaps correctly, that you were simply insisting that your own cultural tradition was superior.

> Physical punishment of children has a long history in Britain. The tradition has included the use of smacking by parents to discipline children and institutionalised corporal punishment within the state education system (until the 1986 Education Act).
>
> Many people have challenged the tradition on the grounds that such behaviour would be unacceptable towards adults so surely it cannot be right to strike children?

Be alert to the source of your opinions

Cultural traditions will influence the practice of early years workers and other professionals. Everyone has to watch out for the misplaced belief that a familiar way of approaching children and childhood is the only right and sensible way.

People often do not question the accepted wisdom of their own culture and time. The unexpected reaction of someone from a different generation or a very different background can make you think.

For instance, Melvin Konner (in *Childhood*, published in 1991 by Little, Brown and Co.) describes how he translated a passage from the 1985 edition of Benjamin Spock's childcare manual for the opinion of a mother from the !Kung San, a hunter-gatherer tribe of Africa's Kalahari desert. She was very disapproving of Spock's advice on how to be busy so as to prevent babies demanding your attention.

You need to examine whether your reservations about a particular way of handling a baby or organising the family diet are mainly because it would not be **your** way.

You might need to ask yourself questions like, 'Is my problem that I don't understand what is going on here?' or 'I was trained very differently but this child seems happy, she's thriving, so what I am worried about?'

A broad base of knowledge and a willingness to allow for different ways is also important in building a picture of the development of an individual child.

> Unless they are restricted by a physical disability, children steadily learn to coordinate vision and fine muscle control. The skills will not show for **all** children through the use of a knife and fork at mealtimes.
>
> This particular skill is still listed in some developmental charts or guidelines. It is far from being a universal method of eating food and would be an inappropriate expectation if a three or four-year-old's family used chopsticks or ate with their fingers.

Taking a full look at children

Children do, of course, vary in how they develop from birth to eight years and how they behave at different ages. However, there are patterns of development or behaviour that are signs that all is going well. Significant variations from the usual patterns and age ranges should catch your attention. Making sense of what you observe or are told about a child has to be a combination of knowledge of child development and a careful assessment of the framework in which that knowledge is being applied.

Part two: Looking at children as a whole

Children are unique individuals. They share much with one another, yet each child has a combination of skills, interests, experiences, feelings and attitudes that will never be repeated as a whole in any other child.

Supporting children's development

Is it possible to define what children need?

All children deserve the support of adults as they grow and develop. Children have a right to enjoy a safe environment which will enable them to learn as they mature towards adulthood.

In society, the adult population will construct a different picture of what children need through the years of childhood. In talking or writing about the needs of children, adults are making judgements about what issues they believe to be most important and appropriate.

What follows is an attempt to describe the main supports to healthy development in childhood, without being unduly swayed by a particular decade or culture. It may well be impossible to discuss the needs of children in any detail without some evidence that the writer is grounded in a particular time and place.

Ensuring children's well being

Children need to be cared for physically

Children's development can be adversely affected unless they have:

- shelter and clothing that protect them appropriately for the climate. In some parts of the world, the potential danger to babies and children is from high temperatures; in other parts it is from extreme cold;

> Social conditions can change the nature of appropriate concern. For example, British publications used to focus on the need to keep children sufficiently warm. The spread of central heating in homes and buildings has led to more specific advice about how warm is warm enough. Such advice has become especially important with the realisation that over-heating may be a factor in the unexplained death of some young babies.

- safety from the risks of physical harm and the extreme stress that results from living in dangerous circumstances – whether the danger is coming from the behaviour of family members or from a society in the throes of war;
- food and water which is safe and nutritious. There are, however, different ways to ensure a balanced and healthy diet;
- physical care and hygiene to keep children healthy from preventable illnesses;
- a combination of sufficient rest and activity in an unpolluted and otherwise safe environment.

Keeping children safe

It is impossible in a book of this length to cover every practical issue relevant to establishing and maintaining a safe environment for babies and children.

You will find a number of pointers and reminders throughout the descriptions of development but you would need to consult other publications for a thorough consideration of safety. You could start with one or two of the suggestions in the further reading section.

Emotional well being

Children's emotional state is closely intertwined with their physical well being. Both will affect healthy development.

Children will not be happy all the time. Sometimes they will be sad or frustrated. As long as distressing or neglectful circumstances do not go on and on, children can be remarkably resilient. Babies and children will flourish when they experience the following circumstances:

- the company and attention of caring adults and of other children;
- affectionate touch and physical closeness that never abuses a child's trust;
- continuity of individual care which combines some predictability for the child with flexibility;
- the security of belonging to a caring family group;
- a sense of personal identity and worth.

Helping children to learn

The story of the first eight years of childhood is a description of just how much children learn in those years.

The under eights are ready to learn

Babies are born with a tremendous capacity for learning. Their senses are working from the first day. As their physical powers mature, anyone who is more than a casual observer will be able to see how much they delight in trying things out. Babies thrill to new discoveries.

Babies and toddlers are fascinated by what are to adults the most ordinary objects and events of life. Young children are excited by exploration; they are naturally curious. They are not unduly daunted by difficulties they encounter, especially if they have learned to be confident in help and encouragement from familiar adults or older children.

So, there is no need for adults to try to persuade very young children towards learning new skills or older children to explore new words or ideas. The task of adults is to encourage rather than discourage children's naturally very high level of interest and desire to learn.

Alison Forbes

Individuality

Children who are close in age may share a similar level of skill or approach to a new situation. Yet they will always react and learn as individuals. So adults have to pay close attention to individual children – what they do and what they say.

You can adjust the amount of help and the kind of information that you give to any child. Your approach needs to vary with their individual abilities and their interests. Children learn best if they are allowed some measure of determining what and how they learn.

Children will investigate play materials with great interest. They will often work out their own way of completing a task or putting their ideas into practice. Children need time to try out different strategies and explore possibilities. Adults will have suggestions but they must respect children's ideas as well – sometimes these will be a new way of approaching a task or considering an idea. Children should be offered direct help if they are becoming frustrated in their efforts. They should also be offered another way of exploring if their preferred method is unsafe or difficult to offer and given a choice of alternative techniques or materials.

A range of experiences

Children benefit from a wealth of different and interesting experiences to enjoy in safety. They learn from the chance to repeat and practise familiar activities, combined with new experiences, people and objects that interest and provoke their curiosity. They enjoy the company of adults and children – not necessarily of their own age.

Potentially, children can learn a great deal in any of the care settings usually available – their own home, a day nursery, a nursery school or playgroup. Any setting will only be as good as the behaviour of the adults responsible for the babies or children. Equipment and play materials do matter, of course, but they will never be an effective substitute for adults who help and support children with affectionate concern.

In many group settings for children the activities on offer will be chosen to build children's experience in different ways and from different emphases. Some planned programme is likely and within the educational system the content is now structured by the National Curriculum. The content and a variety of methods have developed from good practice of recent years.

Building up to skills

Children are often learning a very great deal before the emergence of the skill that adults clearly recognise. For example, children have to grasp a wide range of physical skills and ideas before they will successfully read or write.

When parents and workers recognise this building up to a skill, then they can help children and enjoy with them each step along the way. A very useful piece of thinking for adults can often be to work out what children will need to be able to do or to understand **before** they can possibly achieve a particular physical skill or grasp an idea. For instance, if children have not really noticed the visual difference in shape between round and square, they cannot learn to apply those words to the shapes.

The importance of encouragement

Children look for a response from adults; they want affirmation that an adult has noticed what they have done or said. Their learning will benefit from appropriate information and guidance from adults who know them well as individuals.

Adults support and help children by being generous with the following:

- **Complimentary remarks on what a child has done or said.** This kind of positive input does not have to be spoken words alone. A smile or a hug will sometimes communicate 'Well done' as effectively as talking out loud.

    Children appreciate an individual approach. For instance, they will not feel that they are really being complimented if any child receives the identical words 'That's lovely' or 'Good girl'.

    Sometimes adults communicate that they recognise a child's abilities by showing that they trust him or her to take responsibility for part or the whole of a task. The adults are showing that they value the child's effort and achievement.

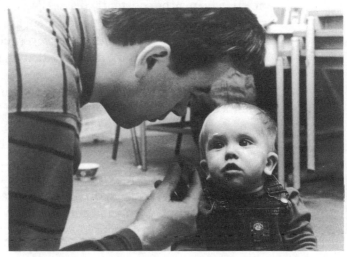

Alison Forbes

Complimentary remarks also include enjoying with a child what he has discovered or made. Babies and children can develop a sense of personal satisfaction. Encouragement helps them realise that they are persevering and exploring for themselves, not solely for rewards in words or treats from someone else.

> Adults need to be careful not to impose their own opinions on children as if these are universally accepted and must be correct. There will often be a number of possible ways of planning and organising a piece of work. Children often discover new approaches precisely because nobody has said 'You must do it this way!' You have to decide by watching children at what point they will benefit from suggestions and when they are asking you for specific information.

- **Constructive feedback to children.** Children are not inevitably distressed by adults pointing out mistakes or by suggestions to do something in a different way. It all depends on how adults behave – on this occasion and in general towards this child.

  For example, children who are never complimented on their efforts or successes, yet whose mistakes are ridiculed, can have almost no confidence in themselves as well as a very negative view of adults. The situation is different for children who have regular experience of adults showing recognition of what they have done and expressing interest and an awareness of the effort that children have expended.

  Children can benefit from adults, and older children, who offer help or give useful information or demonstrations, without taking over. Adults can enable children to appraise their own achievements positively and sometimes to set more realistic goals.

  Adults may need to be especially encouraging of children with special needs, who may be constantly reassessing their achievements against their peers. Children with disabilities can benefit from encouragement in order to develop a positive self image. However, children who are significantly in advance of their peers may feel that their very gifts put them at a disadvantage.

  Adults need to remain sensitive to the difference between praise that genuinely focuses on the child and being patronising. They also need to be aware of the possibility of stereotypes that expect a lower level of skills of one child than another – so that careless work is wrongly praised as being all the child can do.

  In the end, it is not helpful for children to be praised without real thought for their work. Children become aware if any drawing or building is greeted with 'that's nice'. Children of any level of ability do not really benefit from being over-praised for work that is less good than they could probably have managed with more time or effort.

Adults can help children to achieve a **realistic** self image. For example, a child who feels discouraged with his level of football skill may need to be reminded of the high standards he reaches with his detailed maps. A child with physical disabilities may not be able to use her legs for running but she can go fast in her wheelchair and turn with skill when she plays 'touch he'.

Expectations

In any area of development, a child's progress can be influenced by adults' expectations. Children are alert to what adults say or imply by their tone of voice or to which activities they direct a child. So adults' expectations can strongly affect what children will attempt to do or may, in the end, achieve. High expectations can inspire a child, although unrealistically high standards may be daunting. Low expectations may restrict what a child is willing to try or lead children to accept lower than possible standards since adults appear to expect no more.

Adult expectations are sometimes inappropriately affected by stereotypes held of social or ethnic groups, or on the basis of sex.

Helping children

Helping children learn is a challenge for adults. How adults behave and how they speak with children will be very important. Exactly the same words could be spoken by two different adults and yet the first person might, by tone of voice and other body language, convey a very encouraging message and the second could sound grudging and ultimately discouraging.

Children benefit from adults who care and help whilst obviously remaining a unique individual themselves – as are the children.

An important lesson for parents or early years workers is that you will inevitably look back sometimes and feel that you made a mistake or an unwise move. Indeed, adults owe it to children to be willing to realise that they will not always be right. Adults should regard their mistakes in the same way that they encourage children to see theirs – as an opportunity to learn and only as a negative development if the person, adult or child, flatly refuses to consider any other way.

In part three the description of how children develop is divided into different kinds of development. This division has been made to prevent the discussion becoming unwieldy. Of course, learning in the different areas of development blend together for each child. The diagram on page 18 offers one way of looking at the parts that make the whole at any one time for a baby or child.

Viewing children as whole individuals

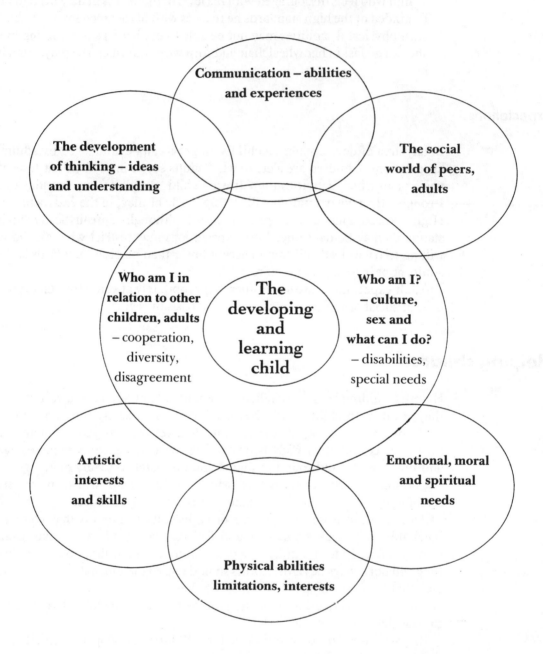

Part three: Development and change from birth to eight years

When you are interested in, or concerned about any child you will need to consider their whole development. You will combine your understanding with the knowledge of other people who also know the child well, or better than you – the child's parents or daily worker. You will be considering how a child is developing in each of the areas of development that are described separately here:

- physical development – the large movements;
- physical development – coordination and the fine muscle skills;
- the development of communication including language;
- the development of thinking and of ideas;
- children's growing ability to take care of themselves and to become active members in a larger community;
- personal and social development – feelings, attitudes and the development of relationships.

In each of the six areas for which development is described, you will find two sections. These are:

- **what happens as children develop;**
- **working positively with children's development.**

The first section describes a **selection** of the changes that you will be able to see as children progress from babyhood to their eighth birthday. The purpose is to give you a good sense of the kind of changes that occur and approximately when.

The second section gives a few practical ideas for how adults can behave in the most helpful way for children as they develop in each area of development. These ideas are relevant to any adult who is spending time face-to-face with babies or young children. They do not pre-suppose any particular setting for children, for example, in a family home or in a school.

They are, once again, only a **selection** of ideas. Some of the suggestions for reading given at the end of the book would be a good source of more comprehensive descriptions of quality care and education of the under eights.

As you read this part to the book, please hold in your mind the following important points about how children develop.

The age at which a skill is achieved will vary

Remember that babies and children vary considerably in exactly when and in what way they learn skills. Any ages given are approximate and will usually be in the form of an age range.

You also need to be aware, or remember that children often appear to come to a temporary halt in one area of development. At any given point in time their development may look uneven. It is actually a feature of early development that children often forge ahead for a while in one or two areas. As with any conclusion about an individual child you will need to take a full look at their development over a time perspective of longer than a week or so.

There will be different patterns of development

Children do not follow identical patterns of development or share the same interests.

For example, children won't run before they have learned to walk but they do not all crawl before they walk. Some walking children are more ready to use their skill than others; some are keen for any willing adult to carry them.

In any group of children you will find that some are more excited or intrigued by particular sources of play material than others. For instance, some children are fascinated from two or three-years-old by making up jigsaws, whereas others exercise the same skills of coordination and experimentation with other play materials.

When should you be concerned?

The material in this book will be helpful if you are feeling concerned about the development of an individual child. The information will support you in gathering your thoughts on a child's level of development and behaviour in play. However, it has not been designed as a diagnostic tool for assessing whether a child is delayed in development or experiencing a disability or learning difficulty.

If you are concerned about an individual child, you will need to bear in mind the following:

- Your general knowledge of children's development – with whom are you comparing this child?
- Your knowledge of this individual child – do you have enough experience of him or her to come to a balanced judgement? If not, with whom do you need to consult?

- Have you consulted with other people who know the child well - parents and daily care workers?
- Are you making sure that you are looking for patterns in this child's behaviour or abilities? Are you being overly swayed by single events or by ways of behaving that appear odd to you?

It is only on the basis of well gathered and considered information on a child that you would be able to decide if your concerns were well founded and then what plan of action should be followed.

Adrian Rowland

Physical development – the large movements

This description of development covers the ability of children in their large movements, such as walking, running or jumping. The second area described takes a focus on children's ability to coordinate the evidence of their senses, particularly vision, with fine physical movements.

What happens as children develop?

Babies

- The physical abilities of very young babies are initially restricted to reflex movements such as sucking.
- Their physical movements look random and jerky and their arms tend to be more active than their legs.
- Because they cannot hold up their heads, they need careful support all along the length of their body. With this support, they can turn their heads. Babies tend to turn in response to a gentle stroking touch.
- Unless affected by disability, babies around three-months-old make smoother movements with their arms and hands, kick vigorously with their feet and can hold their head and neck steady at least for a little while without support.
- By three months all babies take an interest in what goes on around them. Younger babies, who have become more wakeful during the day, will have needed entertaining for some time.

> Cultures around the world vary in how much and in what way babies are carried about by adults or older children.
>
> There has been a noticeable change between generations in Britain. The 1980s saw considerably more use of baby slings and carriers and less of large prams.
>
> Of course, previous generations of parents did not all use prams. Welsh women from the mining villages used to wrap their babies to their bodies with a large shawl.

- By around six months of age, babies are delighting in a much greater control of their own bodies and their explorations are the source of much of their play.
- By about six months, most babies will be able to roll from front to back, lift their head off the pillow, sit upright and look around, although most will need support to stay safely upright.
- Babies' movements are much more purposeful. For instance, they hold up their arms as a request to be picked up. Many babies relish a game of

bouncing up and down when they are held so as to flex their feet against a firm surface.

- By nine-months-old, babies can usually sit unsupported, turning to watch events and reaching out for objects. They can move themselves at surprising speed by crawling or rolling. They may have learned to pull themselves up by holding on to adult hands or convenient furniture.
- One-year-olds will usually be moving about by crawling, bottom shuffling or using furniture as hand holds. They may be walking by now or will be within the next few months. They are becoming more able to move from sitting to standing and to remain steady whilst reaching out for something.

Toddlers — from the first to second birthday

- As babies move into the toddler months, they are learning to walk, climb and begin to run. They have no concept of danger and even in an environment made safe for them, they will sometimes fall. They tend to collide with hard surfaces or stand upright under tables and hurt their head. They can move faster but are not so good at stopping or swerving to avoid people or objects.
- By 15-18 months, toddlers are well able to use their array of physical skills in a sequence which means nothing is safe from this combination of run/climb-and-grab. They explore, experiment and discover as anything takes their interest.
- By 18-24 months, young children have become able to integrate more than one action into an activity. So they can carry an object of interest and still walk along. They enjoy pushing or dragging larger objects, perhaps large wheeled toys.
- They can move from standing to squatting down, climbing up and getting back down at least sometimes. With a safe chance to learn, they may manage to climb up stairs and probably come down by facing the stairs and maybe sliding. They can be in danger of falling if they rush.

  All these skills are possible by the time children are two-years-old. The difference between the physical helplessness of the baby and the speeding toddler is stunning. This full development can be limited by disabilities.

  The world will be a very different place to a partially sighted child. A child who has a disability affecting motor control may be very frustrated in attempts to move and reach for things. Children with disabilities will need additional help, encouragement to persist and sometimes a modified environment to make movement possible or safe.

From two to four-years-old

- Between two and three years children are learning to run well. With the opportunity to learn, this age group can have learned to manage stairs, although they may come down two feet to a step. They begin jumping with two feet together and kicking balls. They are getting adept at climbing; they will apply this skill as enthusiastically on furniture as on a climbing frame.

- Three-year-olds are jumping from low heights, like steps. They have improved their skill in manoeuvering, either on foot or using equipment such as a tricycle. They are adept runners and climbers. They are beginning to be able to balance their weight by standing on one foot for a short while.

- Four-year-olds are adding the skills of running on tiptoe, hopping, confident stair climbing and scrambling over apparatus and up trees with increasing ease.

- Four-year-olds can enjoy games with balls and bats, hoops, bean bags or ropes. They are unlikely to be as confident or accurate in their skills of catching or hitting with a bat as they are in games of running or jumping.

- By five years old, children will run, climb, dance and jump about. Some children combine all these into some hair-raising stunts. Most apply the skills in hiding and chasing games with each other or an involved adult.

Five, six and seven-year-olds

- Six and seven-year-olds become more able to experiment with the movements that they make and deliberately to vary their speed. An enthusiastic adult can interest them in using this skill in expressive moving to music. Some children of six and seven years are stylish dancers – either using rhythm and coordination in their own way to popular music or learning particular forms of classical dance.

- Five-year-olds can probably skip with their feet but it is more likely to be the six and seven-year-olds who learn to use a skipping rope. Once gained, the skipping skill can become part of organised games with individually held ropes or longer ones held by a person at each end. Some of the British skipping chants have passed from generation to generation.

- Five-year-olds can throw a ball, but catching is more difficult, unless the ball is big. They probably catch with their whole arm and not their hands. With practice, six and seven-year-olds can improve their skill at catching and may manage a bat and ball in team games.

- Some five-year-olds can ride a two-wheeled bike but many still need stabiliser wheels. Six and seven-year-olds who persist at the skill can be accomplished bike riders. Yet some children never achieve the necessary balance, or are simply not that interested in bike riding. Previous generations of this age group rode push-along scooters and jumped pogo sticks – two pieces of equipment rarely seen now.

- Six and seven-year-olds become increasingly impressive in climbing and jumping. They learn to suspend themselves – by the arms or hanging by the knees. They may be able to climb a rope or pole, but perhaps not – the coordination involved is quite difficult.

- Seven-year-olds are developing the balance and confidence to walk along a narrow width – on a bench or plank. Given the opportunity, some children become adept on the trampoline or in gymnastics. Some seven-year-olds can swim – even dive. Some have learned to ride a horse. Some seven-year-olds can roller skate. If you visit an ice rink, you will see some six and seven-year-olds who are confident ice skaters, even making low jumps.

Working positively with children's development

Children develop physical skills as they become more and more able to control their bodies. Health and diet also play an important part. The pattern of physical development will also be influenced by a child's level of confidence. These feelings will have been shaped by experiences, including both opportunities and restrictions placed by adults.

Making the most of abilities

Children learn and stretch themselves with the support of adults who encourage them. All children can be helped to feel confident and competent, whether or not they will ever be a real star in the physical arena. Most important, they can be helped to enjoy physical activities and to relish improving their skills.

Children with a sensory or motor impairment will want to explore and develop all possible skills with their friends. Other children can, of course, be discouraging to those with disabilities. However, if adults are actively supportive, children will accept a range of abilities and disabilities in a straightforward manner. It may be the adults who need to avoid being over protective.

Offering a wide range

Beyond the basic skills, children's physical development will be shaped by the activities and equipment that is available and by what they are allowed or encouraged to try.

In Britain, many four and five-year-olds may be learning to ride a bicycle. In other countries, adults may be teaching young children skills that seem a specialised or more adult pursuit in Britain. For instance, families who live close to the mountains in Europe and North America can be teaching three and four-year-olds to ski.

Richard Cloudsley School

Sara Hannant

A chance to practise

There will be a pattern for learning and improving any single skill. For example, children will go through being wobbly on a bicycle before riding smoothly. Once they feel confident in a level of skill, children may well take risks. For instance, riding a bike at speed or with hands off the handle bars.

Any skill benefits from practice and this pattern follows whatever age in years that children first try a skill.

Once children have acquired the basic skills of mobility, they get faster, stronger, more sure of their balance and they start to use these skills in a wider range of physical activities. They get steadily better at those skills that need coordination between different parts of the body – hand and eye for catching balls, legs and arms for skipping with rope.

Children like to repeat the same skill. Partly, they simply enjoy doing something again and again. Repetition is also the way to increased skill and confidence. Adults can encourage a child who has just gained a skill to 'Do it again!' whilst the impetus is still with him or her.

Allowing for individual differences

As they gain full control of their own body, children show particular skills – sometimes real talent – as well as definite likes and dislikes in the physical arena.

Some children have a better sense of balance than others, some pick up coordination skills like skipping faster than others.

Children vary in their level of confidence for physical activities. Some children appear to need more encouragement before they will try any new physical skill; others leap in with a sense of abandon which may unnerve watching adults.

.... but avoiding restrictive expectations

Some three and four-year-olds are alert to messages from adults or other children on what is appropriate for them to try. The over fives can be very strongly influenced by the expressed opinions of adults or other children.

For instance, five and six-year-olds can learn to skip with a rope. However, boys may decide that this skill is not for them, unless they observe a man or older boy, whom they admire, practising the skill.

Some children are more drawn to the large scale physical activities and spend considerably more time on these than other activities on offer. Adults are restricting those children's potential if they assume the children, perhaps energetic boys, can't concentrate so let them run about. This outlook is just as unhelpful as failing to encourage more timid children from stretching themselves physically.

Challenge, interest and safety

Adults caring for babies and children of any age need to give them an opportunity to learn and practise these physical skills in an environment where challenge is realistically balanced with safety.

Babies need to be safe in someone's arms or able to stretch and roll without danger of being trod upon by older children. As babies learn the skills of crawling and later of walking, then their environment needs to be modified to take account of their increased mobility and lack of any understanding of common dangers.

For toddlers, physical development with safety means a safe environment to move around in and a very high level of adult vigilance. Three-year-olds and over still need safety and a watchful adult eye but adults can be at a slight distance.

Mobile babies and toddlers don't get into cupboards, drawers or waste bins with the express intention of being naughty. They do it because the contents are **so interesting**. Any adult's job is to offer the delights of discovery with safe containers and contents.

Even babies enjoy the variety offered by trips out and about. Three-year-olds and older need access to open space for running about and more active play. If a garden is not available, trips will need to be organised to take children out to parks and playgrounds. Otherwise they will practise their physical skills with little regard for wallpaper, ornaments or adult bodies. Some local environments will be potentially less safe for a number of reasons – level of pollution, busy roads or threats from other people, including the risk of racial harassment.

Children will use their physical skills in a certain amount of rough and tumble. Play fighting can certainly get out of hand and some children, especially boys, may have been encouraged to use superior strength to get their own way in a group. Adults have to make a judgement about the point at which they step in to put a stop to unacceptable behaviour.

Variety

Children need the equipment and space to enjoy physical movement and games. Different kinds of equipment may be bought and the natural environment may provide open space and logs or trees to climb.

Three and four-year-olds can organise some of their own games but they appreciate an adult who will join in sometimes as an equal partner in a physical game. Adults offer good company, can demonstrate skills and unobtrusively watch out for safety. Joining in a game can be the most effective way of counteracting stereotypes, such as girls or women don't play football.

As children move towards group games, they also need an adult who will enjoy an activity, whilst keeping a calm hold on the rules of an organised game. Adults need to keep an eye on any physical activity so that nobody is hurt or pressured into dangerous activities through 'dares' – an increasing risk with the over fives.

Activities such as group games and non-competitive games enable all children to learn and develop skills without pressure and will be particularly important for children who may be less confident.

Alison Forbes

Physical development – coordination

What happens as children develop?

Babies

- The focus of the most common fine physical movements are the coordination of eye and hand. At the very earliest stage, babies have to find their hands and develop their visual skills and control. They spread and flex their fingers before they are able to grasp.
- Very young babies gaze intently at the face of a familiar person – parent or other carer – when they are held or fed. They follow slowly moving objects with their eyes.
- By three months of age, babies are deliberately following the movements of adults and children close by. They are equally interested in what they can make their own hands and fingers do. They can firmly grasp a finger placed in their hand but anything else is difficult, although you will observe them persevering.
- By six months, babies are thoroughly curious about any person and happening. They use all their senses in their explorations. They move to reach for interesting objects, using their whole hand to grasp. They explore objects by feel, including putting them into their mouth. They become increasingly adept at making noises by shaking, bashing or dropping objects – using a variety of toys or household objects.
- By nine months they are more able to explore objects in a deliberate way. They turn objects over, poke and sometimes crumple or rip things up. Some objects are dropped over the edge of high chairs or buggies. Given an array of safe objects, babies enjoy separating out and examining the different items, piling them up or banging them together.
- By twelve months, babies have a range of basic skills for exploring what can be done with even small objects and they watch with interest what adults and other children do.
- Babies as young as a few months old can be fascinated by shiny pictures and often scrabble at the image, as if they could get hold of the objects shown. By six or seven months, babies can enjoy being shown picture books, although they are likely to rip paper pages.

Toddlers – one and two-year-olds

- In the second year of life, toddlers become increasingly adept at finding, picking up and using all kinds of objects large and small. They put little objects into larger containers and build piles. Given a set of simple bricks, they may manage a short tower and will then delight in knocking it down.

- Toddlers will use their growing skills within the range of activities available. For instance, by fifteen months, many toddlers can make marks with a crayon or wield a paint brush – if given the chance.
- They watch, with great interest, what adults and older children do. They learn a great deal by copying but they cannot judge whether they are putting themselves in danger by the action they copy.
- By eighteen months, toddlers can have developed a great interest in picture books. They enjoy books with adults, or older children. They tend to turn several pages at a time and like favourite books again and again. Patient adults can teach them not to rip pages.
- They can pick up even little objects with a finger and thumb grasp. By two-years-old, their vision and understanding are sufficient for them to recognise familiar adults in photographs and to identity even small details in picture books.

Three and four-year-olds

Cultures vary considerably in what kind of experiences are judged to be normal to make available for young children. Of course, families vary a great deal within the same culture. You could talk to a range of families in Britain from the same cultural background and still find many differences in what activities they offer their three or four-year-olds.

So, depending on what was made available for them, three and four-year-olds have the potential to become more competent in the following kinds of skills:

- They can really enjoy building with small and larger scale construction material – purchased bricks and other shapes or junk material.
- They will persevere to produce a wide range of drawings and paintings with a variety of shapes that steadily become more recognisable as faces, familiar objects or buildings.
- They can learn to use tools like scissors. They enjoy handling simple craft materials, showing happy satisfaction in what they produce.
- They learn the combination of visual and manipulation skills that are needed to complete jigsaws.

Young children are very motivated to apply their fine physical skills in everyday activities that adults may discount since they do not view them as play.

For example, children enjoy becoming involved in domestic tasks such as real cooking, washing up or tidying and re-organising. Adults may not think to involve children if they find these tasks mundane or tedious. From a child's point of view helping with washing up, for instance, offers the enjoyment of water with bubbles and the satisfaction of doing a grown up task.

John Birdsall

- Physical coordination is needed in many everyday activities - pouring from a jug or juice box, cutting up food, dressing, sticking stamps on letters or handling lots of coins to pay for a purchase at the shop. Younger children will try many of these activities, but four and five-year-olds are becoming more adept at managing them with ease.

Five to seven-year-olds

- You will notice that five and six-year-olds are becoming more able to use their skills with an element of planning. For example, with encouragement, they become more able to think ahead about what they may draw. They can use their language skills to help turn an idea or a two-dimensional plan into a building or a model.
- Over fives become more dexterous in many of the skills described for younger children.

  For instance, five-year-olds will be able to manage most of the fastenings on their clothes, unless these are out of reach at the back. Six or seven-year-olds may still be struggling with shoelaces. Tying laces is difficult, and with velcro on many children's shoes, children may not have had to learn. The same skills of coordination enable children of five, six and seven years to take more responsibility for even the fiddly aspects to their own care. The description of development of self care goes into more detail.

- As with the large physical movements, there will be differences in skill and confidence between individual children. With encouragement, six and seven-year-olds can enjoy putting energy into a special interest or talent that has now emerged from the range of creative or construction activities they have enjoyed as a younger child.
- Their involvement in everyday, domestic activities can be extended by their greater dexterity. For instance, a child of six or seven years, who has been enjoying the weighing and stirring in cooking, may be ready to try to break an egg.
- From five years of age onwards, children can become more trustworthy in the care they take and in following instructions. For example, they become more reliable in watching what they are doing as they pour liquids. Of course, they will still make mistakes or have spills.

  Children who, when younger, were trusted with small parts of a task will now be able to take a larger role in choosing and organising activities.
- Five-year-olds can have confident control over pencils and crayons. You will see an increased level of skill in their drawings. These are much more likely to be recognisable and their abstract paintings or collages can be very creative. Children of six and seven years can wield pencil, crayon or brush to produce a lot of detail in people, buildings or transport.

  They may still use more of a whole hand grip. In order to write, children need to move from a whole hand grasp to a finer fingers-and-thumb hold. They also need to have developed a clear right or left hand preference. Most five-year-olds have a left or right preference.
- Making or copying patterns and pretending to write are important skills that build the basis for actual writing. Some children are able to write before they enter primary school. Generally, children of six and seven years will be learning to write. The skills builds gradually and will not improve without a lot of practice. Children are learning to form letters and get their writing to flow. Gradually, with help, they will learn to spell correctly.

  Bilingual children may be aware of different scripts and directions of writing – English is written from left to right but some other languages, for example Arabic are written from right to left.

Working positively with children's development

A range of activities

Babies and all children benefit from having safe space in which to explore appropriate equipment and materials. They learn from a range of activities and the opportunity to watch adults or older children, joining in as they are able.

Children can learn a positive outlook on the world and people apparently different from themselves when materials and activities represent the wide range of social and ethnic groups within Britain.

Even children as old as six and seven make more mess and general disarray than many adults would ideally like. Patience is needed in tolerating the mess and in motivating children, even toddlers, to help in the clearing up process.

Toddlers in particular will use their skills of coordination in a way that seems indiscriminate, even dangerous, to adults. They are very curious but their fascination can often be diverted from an unsafe activity to a safe one. They can become very absorbed in collections of interesting objects – not all toys – that they can feel, look over and organise in various ways, like putting smaller items into big ones or posting items through tubes or similar shapes.

Trust and encouragement

Adults can be encouraging by words, smiles and other gestures. It is possible to recognise with children, not only the end product or what they have done, but also the thought and effort which they have expended. Three-year-olds and older are also very encouraged when you show you trust them to complete an activity without your hovering over them.

Adults need to check regularly whether they are doing too much for children and not standing back to let them become skilled themselves. Children will take longer and not do such a good job as an adult in some things – until they are allowed to get better.

Children sometimes experience a difficult patch in applying fine physical skills and they can become disheartened. Children need encouragement if they experience a stage when their plans are more ambitious than their current abilities. Some children feel that they must be very good at something very quickly.

Supportive adults can remind children of the progress they have made, perhaps create a private time for practice if at all possible and try to help children to come to terms with the fact that in many skills – not just the physical – there is an uncomfortable stage of being only too aware of what you cannot do rather than what you can.

Showing how

Along with encouragement goes teaching children proper use of tools that will do the job they want, care of equipment and the responsibility of tidying up after yourself. Adults need to remember that there are several stages from

'Let me do that for you' through 'You do it but I will help' to 'Now you do it on your own'. These stages are described in more detail in the section of children's development in self care.

Remember that, when a book such as this describes how six or seven-year-olds are potentially capable of certain skills, this does not mean that children will be able to do it straight away without help or proper supervision for safety.

Monitoring opportunities

Children who have visual or motor disabilities will need extra help to enjoy activities and sensitive modification of the environment to make learning possible. Realistic limitations because of disability must not be a barrier to children's experiencing a wide range of activities. Adults can draw children's attention to the progress that they have made, however small that may be.

Alison Forbes

Adults need to monitor that children are choosing from the full range of activities. Some may feel limited by beliefs that they have heard about 'only girls (or boys) do that'.

It is important in mixed age groups that no age grouping is effectively lost. For example, in a club that has over eights, adults need to recognise that children of five or six years are the younger ones in this setting and can be pushed out by the older children. In a nursery or playgroup setting, three-year-olds can become frustrated with group activities more appropriate for four and five-year-olds – or vice versa, of course.

John Birdsall

The development of communication

The ability to communicate and to understand the communication of other people is central to children's intellectual and social development. Their development includes more than learning recognisable words. Communication includes:

- the learning of a spoken language – for some children, more than one language;
- the growth of understanding of what other people say;
- learning ever more ways of using spoken language, including the skills of conversation;
- attending to the messages from the unspoken body language of others;
- the understanding of written language – again, for some children, more than one language.

Meaning and body language

Adults often underestimate children's awareness of the unspoken messages of the face and body. Many adults assume that, if nothing is said out loud, then children will be unaware of adults' feelings or opinions. In fact these will show clearly through face and body, and can speak louder than words to children.

Just as spoken languages differ, so does body language around the world. Some gestures carry very different meanings in different countries. Children learn the basic rules of non-verbal communication for their culture. Since Britain is a multicultural society, any adult has a responsibility to be aware of cultural differences in body language. Otherwise they can come to unfair conclusions about a child's behaviour or misunderstand adults from a different background.

English and North American culture tends to encourage children to look directly at adults. Avoidance of gaze is sometimes interpreted as evidence that a child has something to hide or is not concentrating.

Such an interpretation is by no means universal. In Japan and parts of Africa, it would be seen as disrespectful for children to hold a direct gaze at an adult.

In the Caribbean, adults sometimes use the expression, 'Don't let your eyes cross me!' – often said to a child being reprimanded. Children learn therefore to look down. People from a different cultural background might misinterpret the behaviour as sullen insolence or evidence of guilt.

What happens as children develop?

Babies

- For very young babies, communication occurs through looks and the comfort of touch, smell and physical closeness. During the early months, babies are expressing their feelings and wants through cries, smiles and a range of sounds and limb movements.

  The sounds made by babies are not specific to individual world languages. As they learn to speak a particular language, their use of sounds is shaped towards the system of the language they are learning.
- By six months of age, babies are producing a whole range of sounds which become playful. They experiment with different rhythms and volume. They can use their sound making and attending skills in a simple conversational exchange with an adult or older child.
- They are very aware of familiar voices and sounds of their daily routine and are curious about unfamiliar sounds. They show their emotions through sounds, cries, chuckles and through their body and face.
- Since babies use both hearing and sight in communicating with others, any doubts about the hearing or visual ability of a baby have to be checked carefully on a separate basis.
- In the second six months of life, babies develop their ability to use sound and body language deliberately – to call for attention, to imitate the sounds made by others, to play around with strings of sound in a tuneful way.
- By twelve months, they are showing an understanding of the basic messages from familiar others – the names of family members, a few everyday names of objects in context, a firm 'No!'

Toddlers – one and two-year-olds

- Touch and physical closeness remain important for children. Affectionate touch is a clear message of caring as well as one way to attract a child's attention. Touch will be especially important when babies are found to have visual or hearing disabilities.
- In the second year of life, toddlers learn steadily to express their wants and to understand what other people – adults and children – are communicating to them.
- From one to two years, toddlers' understanding and use of actual words is increasing. They do not depend solely on spoken words since they also make sense of any communication from the context in which the words are spoken.

  They have working theories of what adults, or children, are likely to be saying or asking. They are also alert to body language – for example, gestures and the direction of someone's gaze. Using this whole communication, they become able to follow simple instructions and to find and show a whole array of everyday objects, toys and parts of their own body.

- In the months up to two years, they will most likely start to use words and simple phrases that are understandable to adults and children who know them. They use gesturing and repetition to push the message home. They may enjoy rhymes and simple songs and join in.

- Although children vary, it is realistic to expect communication through speech by two years of age or soon after that birthday.

> Children's mistakes in spoken language are often sensible conclusions that they reach from what they have heard so far.
>
> For instance, an 18-month-old boy was calling water 'more'. His mother realised that, when he came to the back door to have his toy watering can refilled, she was asking, 'Do you want some more?'

Children of two, three and four years

- In the twelve months from two to three years of age, children usually have a growing vocabulary that can be approaching a couple of hundred or several hundred words. They can put these words together to form short sentences and they begin to ask simple questions.

- If children are taken seriously in what they say, they will want to communicate, even though they do not know all the words they need. They use the language they have learned and fill in any gaps with gestures. Children who feel confident that adults are interested in what they have to say will persevere and try other ways to convey their messages.

- It is not unusual for two and three-year-olds to stop and start in their flow of speech. They have to gather their thoughts and are often trying to express something for which they do not have all the words. Any feeling that they must hurry or else they will have lost an adult's attention can lead to a kind of stuttering.

- Many children chat to themselves in play as well as to an adult or child listener. Children develop their own creative use of grammar and pronunciation. They may make up their own words. Less frequently, children who are emotionally very close to one another – for instance twins – have created an exclusive language that only they can understand.

- Many children of two and three years have a delight in music and simple musical instruments. They often enjoy being part of a singing or rhyme session, whether or not they want to perform.

- Three and four-year-olds use their vocabulary in sentences that convey a wide variety of messages – requests, questions, telling about, recounting stories, arguing – and can be able to hold a simple, turn taking conversation. They use their language skills in imaginative play.

Sara Hannant

- Their language extends as they listen to other adults and children and watch what goes on. They incorporate words and ideas from what they encounter from books or programmes on television.
- Some children of three and four years are becoming fluent in more than one language. They may be learning two languages at the same time, or learning a second some time after the first.
- Three and four-year-olds will learn the more general behaviour of communication. For example, how much and how patiently children will listen tends to be influenced by how their own communications are received. Children who are interrupted or shouted at will tend to copy this way of behaving. They can learn swear words or offensive terms as easily as any other speech. It is possible for a patient adult to discourage children from using language which is unacceptable to that adult.
- Children can use words to define the meaning of other words, which shows a good grasp of the abstract. Younger children can point out a picture of a ball or show a real ball, but it is the older child (often four-years-old and up) who can give a definition in words.
- Children can use their speech to talk about not only what is happening now, but also about the past and the future. Their time perspective is not yet an adult one; they do not have enough information.

- Children with sensory and communication disabilities may need specialised equipment and skills, such as sign language, in order to express themselves – both now and as they get older.

Children of five, six and seven years

- By five years old children have a very large vocabulary. Listing all the words a five or six-year-old can use and understand would be a major project. Children will recognise words that are new to them and often ask for the meaning.
- From five years on, children will be able to use their words for many different purposes. They can use language to describe, to question, to wonder about and guess, to explain, to justify or to complain. They can have learned a wide use of language.
- Six or seven-year-olds can be persistent questioners, sensing if they have only been given half an answer. They are able to reason logically with the support of language – both speaking out loud and thinking ideas out in their head with internal speech. They can plan, speculate and think ahead within the limits set by what they already know and have experienced. The section on the development of thinking returns to this area.
- Children of five and six years can hold a long conversation with another child or an adult with whom they feel comfortable. The key point about conversation is that it involves turn taking, listening to another person and saying something yourself that links in with the general topic.
- Five-year-olds have the flexibility with their spoken language to vary their voice and choice of words to play a part in imaginative play with other children. Children of six and seven years who play together on a regular basis develop rich imaginative play sequences, often returning to established roles and actions from the point these were left some days earlier. They may create simple roles for younger children who might not instigate such complex play sequences without support.
- By six and seven years some children can be showing a striking talent for acting and expressive dance or mime.

    Six and seven-year-olds are exploring the boundaries between fact and fantasy. They may become slightly confused on occasion but many seven-year-olds are ready to sort out acting from reality in television programmes.
- From five years of age, children continue to expand their abilities to express themselves. If encouraged, they become confident to express opinions and to support their views. Once again, there can be cultural differences in how children are expected to behave. If obedience and compliance are valued above individual expression of ideas then it may be considered disrespectful for children to challenge the views of a teacher or parent.

If adults are patient in listening, six and seven-year-olds can be more able to express their emotions in words – what they are feeling and something about the reason.

- Children remain alert to what is said through body language, although they are less dependent on this source of information to understand communication. Children are not necessarily any more coherent in explaining their feelings about others than are many adults.

- Children of five, six and seven years have a great capacity to remember if their interest has been engaged and they are encouraged to practise. They can learn poems, songs and parts in simple dramatic productions. The same ability to learn and remember means they can be taught, bit by bit, important information like their full name, address and, where appropriate, telephone number.

- Children have different kinds of conversations with each other than with adults. Seven-year-olds, for example, enjoy gossip that they would not tell adults and chat at length about topics that they guess – possibly correctly – would not especially interest their parents or teachers.

- The way children over five years use their words in total communication will depend on the adult or child models that they copy. Have they learned to expect that adults will listen to children or answer their questions? Have they experienced enjoyable conversations with adults or their peers?

- Five and six-year-olds' speech is fluent and mainly correct according to the language they have heard spoken. Adult speech comes in stops and starts and is often not strictly grammatically correct. Children will accurately produce the local accent, their family accent, or be learning to move flexibly between the two.

- The fluency of multilingual learners will depend, of course, on how long they have been learning each language and the extent of support and practice for each.

- Normally five and six-year-old children will be able to pronounce the majority of the sounds of their language. A few problems with sounds are not unusual. For instance, in English, the more difficult sounds tend to be the groups of s/f/th and r/l/w/y.

- Children with communication difficulties need particular help, often from specialists – speech therapists and specialist teachers. The use of signing, communication boards and computers will often be the key to allowing children to develop and increase their knowledge of the world around them.

  Any such developments will always need to be progressed in partnership with the children's parents.

- By five years, some children are already well aware that words can also come in a written version. They may be recognising some familiar words such as their own name or a well known high street store. Some may actually be able to write and read.

Within the age span from five to eight years, many children are capable of learning to read and write. There will be wide individual differences in their level of skill by eight years of age. Children who have been given plenty of attention and who are still struggling may have a specific learning difficulty. They are likely to need more specialised help that takes account of the difficulty they are experiencing and which will support their level of confidence.

Working positively with children's development

Giving time – showing interest

Children's language benefits enormously from the attention of patient and encouraging adults who give generously of their time and show a genuine interest in what babies and children are communicating. The rich array of play materials and books can support but will not effectively take the place of an involved adult.

From birth to eight years, children will flourish with close and affectionate contact with adults who model considerate behaviour in communication.

Very young babies want adults to be close, making contact by touch and look. In the early months of life, babies need the communication of sounds and smiles and a timing from adults that gives the baby a chance to respond.

Toddlers warm to adults who will pay attention to the child's ways of communicating and be patient as they express themselves. Toddlers, like babies, need adults who will give opportunities for a genuine two-way exchange and let the child lead the exchange sometimes.

Showing how

Adults show children the kind of behaviour that they expect. Children will copy an adult who listens and pays attention to a child in the way that he or she wishes to receive from that child. Babies and children learn the turn taking of conversation from adults who guide and show a genuine interest in what excites the child, as well as introducing new topics.

An adult who respects a child's level of language and ideas can repeat a word or phrase so that a child can hear a correct pronunciation or another way of expressing an idea. Children who are generally encouraged by adults will learn in this way. Children will be disheartened by adults, or older children, who ridicule their mistakes or bluntly correct them.

Children enjoy the company of adults who will have conversations with them on a wide range of topics and who will listen to their troubles and worries as well. Children will drift away from adults who want to do all the talking or who rarely show enthusiasm for any of the children's own interests.

Understanding the tasks

Children deserve adults who will take the time and trouble to look through three, five or seven-year-old eyes to grasp what it is that the child does not understand, and to offer a breadth of experiences for the children.

It helps if adults have some understanding of the process involved and if they make the effort to recall what it was like as a child not to know a skill or idea.

For example, six and seven-year-olds may be able to read words that they cannot reliably spell. These are two different tasks. When children write their own material, they have to recall how to write and spell a word, they have to summon it up from their memory. When they read, they have to recognise a word. Recall and recognition are different.

A positive environment

Adults are important in creating an environment in which communication skills are encouraged and children have relative peace in which to exercise their skills.

For instance, children benefit from the company of other children – younger, a similar age or older. However, adults may be the ones to ensure that the noise level does not get out of hand or to show that differences of opinion do not have to turn into fierce arguments.

Children of four and five years and older need a wide range of reading and writing materials. They are encouraged to concentrate when they have a quiet area or room to spread out their work, to think and to practise their growing skills.

Bilingual children need the opportunity to read in both of their languages. It is possible that they are more fluent in their first language and it will be very important that they have the books for practising their reading skill.

Children will benefit from adult attention and support appropriate to the level of skill that they have gained so far. They will learn with adults who will listen to them read, correcting any mistakes with patience and kindness. Children like adults to continue to read to them, even when the children can read to themselves. Books can also be explored as part of a group – perhaps through drama.

Children have great capacity to learn and to persevere with complex skills like reading and writing. With encouragement they will experience great satisfaction as they deal with this challenge.

Adrian Rowland

Some young children have learned to enjoy books and are very excited about the prospect of being able to read and write. Sometimes it will be especially important that adults show children that written material is all around them — not only in books.

Adults can help through everyday activities. For example, reading instructions on a packet, reading street names and the names of shops, making shopping lists or notes.

Alison Forbes

The development of thinking

At the same time that they are developing physical skills and communication, children are also expanding their understanding of how the world works.

Spoken language opens up a whole new world to children and their use of words is often the way for adults to understand how the child is now thinking. Babies and very young children are also developing working theories about the world around them. An observant adult can make a shrewd guess by watching what a very young child is doing.

What happens as children develop?

The under threes

- Babies' five senses are working from birth. Within the limits set by their physical abilities, very young babies are exploring and absorbing information.
- Babies learn within the early months the boundaries between their own body and the rest of their world. Their physical explorations provide experience of the simple laws of cause and effect. Babies sometimes learn the effects of their own actions when they bite their own toes, or inadvertently hit themselves with a rattle.
- Within the early months, babies learn to recognise familiar and unfamiliar noises and voices and behave differently. They come to know the sounds of a routine activity like bathtime and, if they like the activity then they will show pleasure in anticipation.
- Within the first year of life, babies work out a vital aspect to the world – things and people are not gone for good if you cannot see them. They learn to search for toys that have been hidden.
- Depending on their experience, by about a year old, babies have worked out some probabilities for their own life – a shout usually brings an adult, a smile brings a smile in return, objects dropped over the side of a highchair are often picked up by an adult.

  Toddlers expand swiftly on these basics, discovering some further rules about how the world works. Some of these discoveries will be with delight – what you can do with water, the fun of finding out how something fits together. Since toddlers have no sense of danger, other discoveries may be uncomfortable – hot things can hurt, cats sometimes scratch.
- If you watch, it becomes obvious that toddlers can remember and use their memories. Young children do not recall everything that an adult asks them to do, nor do they necessarily wish to follow the instruction that they remember.

Juleigh Gordon

The ability to recall and use the experience of previous days now helps the toddler and even more so the two and three-year-olds, who start to grasp some simple ideas about the world around them. Two and three-year-olds have little grasp of the concepts of danger, of time or of sharing – as adults mean them. The different outlooks of child and adult can be a source of friction where an adult does not realise or is reluctant to look through a child's eyes.

Although adults need to observe the behaviour of older children, once their language has progressed, the children often will say something, or ask a question that gives a hint about how they now understand and make sense of the world.

Children of three, four and five years

Three and four-year-olds are coming to terms with a whole range of abstract ideas. Some of these ideas, such as size or shape, can be described in words that relate to qualities that can be seen or touched. Other ideas, for instance, about emotions or concepts like fairness, are described in words but are not tangible.

Children's growing ability to think and reason about other people and their behaviour is closely linked with their feelings and the pattern of their family relationships and friendships. Look also at the section on personal development.

The growth in children's understanding varies a great deal. The pattern of **what** they learn and **when** they finally understand an idea will depend on their interests and the experiences they are offered. A crucial factor in children's experience will be how much and how well adults explain and patiently help children to grasp what are complicated ideas.

In the same way as the descriptions of other areas of development, what follows is only a **brief selection** of what children are learning.

- Between three and five years of age, children are usually interested in other people – what they look like and how they behave. They are becoming aware of the differences between the sexes and the visual signs of different ethnic or cultural identity. Their view of these differences can be solely descriptive, it is not inevitably positive or negative. Five-year-olds can still be assuming that all or most families operate like their own.

- Children of three, four and five years are forming friendships – sometimes with children younger or older than themselves. If they have experience of being in a group, like a nursery or playgroup, they will be coming to terms with the idea that other children sometimes do or say things that hurt and they will be learning strategies to respond to this.

- They are working to understand the behaviour of others and the rules of what is expected of them. They are finding that not all adults have the same definition of politeness and rudeness. Four and five-year-olds can be more capable of recognising that other children and adults have feelings too. The development of their powers of thinking and reasoning is intermingled with their emotions.

- Children of four and five years are sorting out some basic ideas about right and wrong, although at this age they may simply accept the definition of an adult whom they respect and who treats them with affection. They understand the idea of rules for behaviour and can follow simple reasons. They may be accepting that not all adults apply the same rules.

  Children in this age group can look visibly shocked when they encounter children who do not obey the rules that they have assumed are universal. For instance, children who have been taught not to hit out discover that hitting or biting is the first reaction to frustration from some other children.

- From three-years-old children are becoming more and more interested in their own environment and how this changes. They are starting to understand differences in the weather and the changing seasons. They can be intrigued by animal and plant life but understand only a little about how easy it can be to hurt pets or damage plants.

- Three or four-year-olds are often very interested in babies and in hearing about their own development. Stories about their babyhood, or that of known adults, and photos often holds their attention in conversations and projects.

- Three and four-year-olds are often fascinated by watches and other time pieces. They can be learning some understanding of times of the day, since they link ideas of time and time passing to routines and usual happenings.
- Three-year-olds can be interested in numbers and may enjoy counting up real objects or counting up to as far as they can go. Four and five-year-olds will have learned many number names and the order in which they go 1,2,3,4,5 and so on. They may be able to count up to 20 or 30. With practice they can have learned that, when counting actual objects or people, you stop counting when you have run out of items.
- Four and five-year-olds are becoming able to classify examples of a larger grouping. For example, they may understand that cats or dogs are different kinds of animals. Children's special interests will be reflected in their conversation and individual five-year-olds may show a detailed knowledge of a topic that has fascinated them – cars, dinosaurs or flowers.
- Three and four-year-olds initially make direct comparisons of obviously different looking objects. They start to develop ideas about basic measurement and different ways of comparing by overall size. Initially, they think in terms of relatively 'big' or 'little'. Through experience, four and five-year-olds begin to distinguish different kinds of 'bigness' – for example, by height or weight, and to start the process of using words that discriminate more finely (tall, short, fat or thin.)
- Three and four-year-olds are becoming able to distinguish the different characteristics of concrete objects and to use the words to describe these. They are learning about the feel of objects, their overall shape or colour and characteristics such as whether an object is likely to float or sink in water. They discover the implications of different qualities, for instance, that you can do different things with wet and dry sand. Children continue to explore and learn about the natural world if they are offered a breadth of play activities and experiences.
- They are becoming aware of concepts like distance – in relative terms such as near or a long way away. They often grasp basic differences like temperature and relative speed in terms of the extremes – hot or cold, fast or slow.

Children of five, six and seven years

By five years of age, children can have a broad grasp of concepts about the world around them. Much will depend on the experience they have had in their early years. They do not necessarily use the correct words. They can still be confused about ideas that seem very obvious to adults.

Some six and seven-year-olds can be sufficiently interested in a topic that they explore it independently, through books and television programmes. Children can then share information that is genuinely new to adults who have not had the same interest in particular animals or technology.

Just as toddlers adore exploring with their physical skills, so over fives can use their language skills to explore ideas – often through posing questions. A wide range of topics can interest children – from the philosophical 'What happens when someone dies?' to the apparently mundane, but so far unexplained, 'Why do the pipes in my bedroom make such a noise?'

- Five or six-year-olds may have enough experience to understand now that not all people share their opinions or that families differ in life style or the family members who live in the same home.
- They express opinions and preferences. Sometimes friendships may be disrupted by serious differences of opinion. Over fives sometimes try to puzzle out, or are distressed by the apparent unpredictability of their friends' behaviour.
- Children from five to seven years encounter more examples of different ground rules and may begin to question the behaviour of adults that runs counter to those adults' own rules. They are developing a working idea about fairness and justice. In judging the behaviour of other children or of adults they are more able to take into account what someone intended rather than focusing solely on the outcome.
- Most over fives are interested in but are often confused about the events of life. Some four or five-year-olds have already cross-questioned adults on the facts of birth or death; others may have asked few questions at all on the topic.

  They are now learning more accurate information about babies and growth. Five to seven-year-olds are also building an understanding of relative health and sickness, of growing up and growing old and of relative ability and disability.
- Children from five to seven years learn more about animal and plant life and the conditions that both need to flourish. They can be aware and concerned about their local environment. From being able to recognise and describe changes in the weather, six and seven-year-olds may ask detailed questions about what causes events like storms or rainbows.
- Five or six-year-olds can be more aware of clock time but telling the time may prove a challenge even for seven-year-olds. They can be starting to learn but many will still be confused over some aspect – not least because they have to grasp time shown by clocks with hands and digital time, both 12 and 24-hour.

  They have a more sophisticated grasp of time as in past, present and future and can become interested in historical projects – local or international.

- Five-year-olds should be clear about simple, practical applications of number – fetching a specific number of objects, counting how many with accuracy, recognising small quantities without having to count one-by-one.

  Five and six-year-olds will become confident in recognising and writing numbers. Six and seven-year-olds can be making sense of operations of adding or subtracting and some may be able to do simple calculations in their head. They will have some understanding of money and calculations involving coins.

  The development of children's understanding of number is considerably more detailed than covered here. Some references at the end of the book could help you with more detail if you wished to know about how maths, and other subjects are taught in primary school.

- From five years of age children extend their understanding of concepts like size, shape, weight, and dimensions of height and breadth. They become more confident about the words to describe different qualities and explore ways of measuring. They are using their growing understanding of maths in practical activities like measuring or weighing.

- Six and seven-year-olds are extending the grasp of concepts that they gained in their earlier years. For example, their recognition of different shapes may now extend to understanding properties of different shapes like corners or whether a 3-dimensional shape will roll. They can be intrigued by basic scientific principles and are beginning to understand what happens to everyday materials if they are, for instance, soaked or heated.

- Five-year-olds are usually clear about distinguishing colours one from another. Any child who is still confused after patient help, should be assessed for the possibility of colour blindness.

Working positively with children's development

Sharing a child's interests

Babies and children are best helped by adults who become excited with them about their discoveries and their achievements. Adults can only do this if they join with children in play and remain close enough to be able to observe what children are doing and what interests them. Because they come to ideas fresh, children can delight adults with new insights. Adults can successfully extend and build on a child's current interests.

Try to see the world through children's eyes

Children benefit, as in all other areas of development, from adults who will be patient and encouraging. As with language development, a key point in approaching a child's thinking is to take the time to work out what a child does not understand.

Even with a shared spoken language, adults may sometimes struggle to ascertain the point at which children are getting lost in an idea. Are the children themselves confused or are they having trouble making an adult understand an idea which is actually very clear to them?

Children are developing their skills of reasoning and will work to make sense of information on the basis of what they understand so far. Since children still have a great deal to learn, their reasoning skills will sometimes lead them to logically sound yet wrong answers. The effort to explore a child's mistakes is often the key to finding out the source of their confusion and therefore how best to help them.

Children are helped by adults who are prepared to return to the basics of an idea when a child is confused and not assume automatically that the child is being awkward. Some ideas and ways of describing the world only seem obvious to adults because they have lived with these ideas for many years. It is far from obvious to a child, who may also have used four-year-old reasoning skills to reach a conclusion that is logical only given a four-year-old information base.

Adults can watch out for children who are getting stuck with any idea. Children can become disheartened or show a lack of interest because of unresolved confusions. Expectations can also play a part in how far children will persevere. Adults need to make sure that they do not conspire in the idea that certain groups of children, for instance girls, are naturally less good at maths or science. They may need to take specific action to emphasise that both boys and girls can be equally good at such tasks.

Willingness to seek additional advice

Careful assessment by specialists may be required to understand the stage of development of children who are unable to communicate through spoken language. Appropriate intervention and support can be necessary to ensure that children's learning can progress.

Children are poorly served by an approach that assumes problems will just clear up. If sensitive adults have offered a lot of support and time, then either the support is inappropriate or the persistent learning difficulties may need more specialist help.

Learning through play

Adults can support children's learning and are responsible for making sure that children have a wide range of suitable activities and materials to explore and a safe environment in which to play. However, adults do not need to set out to tell or show children everything they need to learn. Children are naturally interested and motivated to explore through play unless they have specifically been discouraged. They will apply their existing skills and by using play materials will extend those skills and discover more about the world.

For example, babies learn with delight about different sights, sounds, tastes, textures, temperatures and smells by staring at familiar faces, at rattles and mobiles and other toys as well as from natural and other household objects. They explore different sensations in finger play with adults and by sucking toys and other safe materials. Adults help by providing the toys and the physical play and by bringing babies who are not yet mobile to see and feel interesting and safe objects. (see Elinor Goldschmied's video on 'treasure baskets' listed in 'Further reading').

Alison Forbes

Toddlers will learn as they persevere to put one object into another, perhaps with a set of nesting boxes, and discover by experimenting that sometimes the first object is too big or that it will only fit one way round. Adults can help by offering a range of play materials that enable toddlers to explore the same basic principle with different objects.

Children will often be learning and practising several different skills within one enjoyable play activity. For example, a small group of three-year-olds may be doing hand prints with an adult. They could be learning how a firmer hand press makes a clearer print and how the different paints blend to form new colours. At the same time they could be using their communication skills as they talk both with each other and the adult. They could additionally be learning how to wait a short time to get their turn.

Children learn with and alongside other children. They also benefit from the input of adults who both talk and listen and who are prepared to show what they mean and not depend entirely on words to carry some very complicated ideas.

Children can develop their understanding of abstract ideas and the world around them through play activities and the wide range of games available. Trips out and about can supplement the possibilities of the indoor and outdoor environment where children spend most of their days.

Adults can draw on a wide range of play equipment, materials and books. These can be supplemented from different sources to provide posters, video and selected television programmes, tapes and computers where available. Through the selection and an effort to extend resources, adults can help children to see and understand the world beyond their own immediate neighbourhood. Such materials can also support a positive attempt to introduce all children to the differences within a multicultural society and to challenge such prejudices as emerge.

There are so many exciting books and work programmes that adults can help children take different approaches to the different areas of learning. The many software packages offer another approach to many subjects. Community resources such as libraries can add to the resources of a school or playgroup.

Although children have not changed, the availability of technology has changed dramatically in the last decade. This generation of under eights are more at ease with computers, at a younger age, than their parents. Adults can demonstrate to children that computers and video links are effective and enjoyable for much more than quick reaction games. Adults in charge of a group may find they have to monitor carefully that all children gain equal access to the computer. There does seem to be a real risk that boys can dominate computer time and girls may hold back, unless an adult supervises sensitively.

John Birdsall

The growth of self care and responsibility

Children and growing up

The under eights are slowly moving into more grown up ways of behaving. Part of this development is that they become less dependent on adults for their physical care and guidance in the details of everyday life. This section is a description of what can be possible as children develop the physical coordination and ability to think ahead that supports their taking on more responsibility.

Seven-year-olds are not completely independent people. They still need care and protection as well as help in some everyday tasks. Six or seven-year-olds are capable of taking responsibility for some aspects of their own life and care and are often pleased to be trusted to do so. In a group they are ready to share in aspects to care and organisation. A thoughtful adult can involve much younger children.

> Different cultures and social groups vary in what the adults expect and train children to be able to do by the age of seven or eight. You may like to think over whether Western society has cut off children too much from adult activities. Children's play and their choices between activities show how much they wish to be a real and respected part of family and work life.

Any concerned adult will always have to judge whether a child's capabilities are being abused. The fact that many six and seven-year-olds around the world do survive living on the streets or spend their waking hours in hard, stressful jobs does not mean that such a situation is an acceptable way to treat children.

What happens as children develop?

Babies

- Very young babies need all the tasks of physical care done for them. Although often tiring for the adult concerned, this apparently ceaseless round of feeding and changing is a precious time of physical closeness and communication for babies.
- By six-months-old, babies can be taking part in their routines – making efforts to feed themselves, holding a bottle or feeder cup, pushing their arms into a sleeve held out for them.

- From the baby's perspective, the activity is in the spirit of play rather than self-help. So, food is as likely to be flicked at the cat as go into the baby's mouth and an arm will be pulled out of a sleeve as well as pushed in.

Toddlers

- One-year-olds can often drink without assistance from a cup and can feed themselves to an extent if adults are tolerant of the mess. If they are in the mood, they can cooperate in dressing by aiming their arms and legs into the lined up clothing held by an adult.

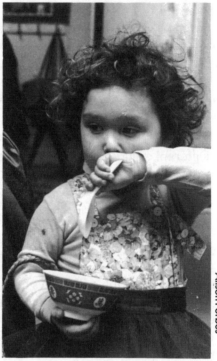

Alison Forbes

- From one to two years, toddlers get better at handling cups, and getting their food into their mouths. If they are provided with a spoon, they learn to scoop up food and reach their mouths with most of the contents. Mealtimes are still usually fairly messy, if toddlers are encouraged to eat and drink without an adult insisting on taking over.

  Neither babies nor toddlers should be left alone when they are eating or drinking – the chance of choking is too great.
- Some toddlers become aware of the physical signs that mean they are about to urinate or pass a bowel movement. Some can be fairly reliably toilet trained for daytime by two years of age. Achievement of this control is very variable. Some 18 to 24-month-olds seem blissfully unaware of what is happening below the waist.

- Toddlers are often interested in involvement in domestic activities. Adults who offer a small and safe task will build the basis for growing skill as children's physical coordination and ability to follow instructions develops.

Children of two, three and four years

- Even young children enjoy having a role in decision making. Toddlers like making choices between activities on offer. Three and four-year-olds can be ready to add their opinion to a more general discussion about what could be done or how. It is important that adults take up on some of the children's suggestions.

Sara Hannant

- Two-year-olds become more adept at eating, with less spillage. They learn to manage simple bits of their clothing - hats and pull on shoes. They may be able to pull pants or loose trousers down but probably not back up again.
- Two-year-olds are usually ready to be toilet trained for daytime. The whole process usually takes months, not days or weeks, before children are reliably trained. Even children who are very motivated will have accidents. Some three and four-year-olds can still be distracted by absorbing play or simply leave it too long before they go to the toilet.

- Much depends on what is expected of children and the pressures on adult carers. Some two and three-year-olds manage a great deal in feeding and dressing themselves, since there has been little option but to get on with it. Hard-pressed parents or workers responsible for a group of young children should remember that they are asking a lot of this age group. It is not surprising if young children really want an adult to do something for them. If help is available sometimes then children can enjoy being self reliant at other times.

- Three and four-year-olds have become capable of many of the tasks of feeding themselves, managing in the toilet, and dressing. They may still need, or appreciate some help sometimes. They can have learned basic hygiene of washing and simple self care, for example, brushing their hair.

- From two or three-years-old, children are increasingly able, and interested, to take on manageable roles in the daily organisation of a home or a group. They will enjoy fetching and carrying, laying tables, doing some washing up, tidying or sorting out. Two and three-year-olds may be able to take responsibility for the simpler parts of preparing a snack or organising drinks. Children of three and four years can take a simple verbal message to someone in another room. Even younger children will enjoy trying to take a message.

- Children with disabilities may have difficulties in extending their skills in some areas of self care. Adults will need to look carefully at how best to help the children learn.

Five years and older

- Children over five years old can usually dress themselves, feed themselves and manage without help in the toilet if the adults responsible for them have expected that they learn to do things this way. They can wash and bath themselves, but probably not to adult standards and therefore need help and some checking on teeth and hair.

    They will learn the rules of their own culture about hygiene, for example, any pattern of which hand is used for different tasks of personal hygiene. As with any kind of learning, children need to be reminded and practise for a habit to become part of their life.

    From five to seven years children have usually managed the remaining difficult fastenings on their clothes. They do not all learn to dress or change their clothes at speed, nor does their choice of clothes for the day necessarily meet adult approval.

- The majority of five-year-olds are fully toilet trained during the daytime. Most will also be able to sleep through an entire night without accident. Some five-year-olds may still be lifted and taken to the toilet when their parent or other carer goes to bed.

    Some children will have a disability that makes incontinence a part of life. They will want to take on such aspects of their care as they are able. Adults should help children discreetly and help them maintain the privacy that matters to older children.

Children with no obvious disability but who are not toilet trained daytime, or night time, need some specialist help. They and their families will need support and advice to work out the best approach to resolve the problem.

- Most five-year-olds will be able to feed themselves by the method of eating used by their families – whether that is chopsticks, fingers, knives and forks, or spoons. Any difficulties left will depend very much on how much of the cutting up has been done as the meal was prepared. Six and seven-year-olds may still need some more help on cutting up meat, or getting poultry off the bone.

- Children of five and six years have the physical skills to serve out food and to feed themselves with very little adult help. They do sometimes of course drop food by mistake or shoot it off their plates. Children vary a great deal in how fast they eat and their likes and dislikes.

  They will have learned what adults expect of them by way of table manners and will be able to behave differently in different settings according to the adult's expectations.

- Children over five years who have been given a role to play in daily organisation can be a great help. Children can gain personal satisfaction from being trusted to carry out some tasks without close supervision. They may now know all that is needed to lay tables for meals or to get out particular activities.

- Children can now be reliable takers of messages or adept finders of lost play items. They enjoy making decisions between possible activities and being involved in planning trips.

  It is important that adults trust six and seven-year-olds to undertake a wider range of tasks. Adults will continue to have to balance up whether children are able to do something against whether it is safe to allow them. For example, six and seven-year-olds can be as fascinated as younger children with baby care. Boys and girls may be great helpers but should not be left in charge, however much they may want.

- Some six or seven-year-olds are becoming ready to speak up for themselves at a doctor's or dentist's appointment. A parent or other carer can be ready to supplement the information.

- Young children can learn a concern for the environment and reflect this concern in how they behave. As with any other development, you will see a progression in how their behaviour develops and their ability to understand and then explain the reasons for behaving this way rather than any other.

  For instance, toddlers may put their litter in a bin because they are being cooperative with an adult's wishes. Toddlers also like putting small things into larger containers. Children of five or six years can have understood the consequences of irresponsible behaviour like dropping litter and will model themselves on adults they respect.

Working positively with children's development

Providing opportunities

Children's development from total dependence towards self care is linked to whether they are yet physically able to do tasks for themselves. Equally important is whether the adults who care for them both encourage and let the children learn to do things for themselves.

Young children make next to no distinction between what adults may see as playtime and the everyday tasks that they want children to practise and learn eventually to do for themselves. Indeed, in many cultures adults would be surprised by the Western idea of children's play as an activity separate from the rest of family and adult life.

Adults need to give space and time for children to have a safe and manageable part of an adult domestic activity. For children to learn, adults have to be flexible about how fast a task is completed and to what standard.

Encouragement

Children can be well motivated to become self reliant. However, they will not be attracted to becoming less dependent if the reality is that then adults flatly refuse ever to help. A moralistic stance of 'You can do it, so get on with it' is discouraging and unfriendly. Considerate behaviour between adults includes offering to do something, like get a drink for more than just yourself, which the other adults are physically capable of doing.

Children deserve compliments for their growing abilities and trustworthiness. They will learn with standards that challenge but are not unrealistically perfect. They will also learn as adults take a range of opportunities to help children to learn.

Children also like and deserve positive recognition beyond the time when they have first gained a skill. Encouraging a child to try turns into complimenting them on how well they can now complete a task. Then the appropriate positive remark may be to thank them for taking a responsibility or express pleasure in how they can be trusted.

Children need opportunities to make decisions and gradually develop a sense of self-determination. Part of this growth is accepting the consequences of one's own actions and, with adult help, trying to put right any mistakes or spills. Children can experience a boost to their self-esteem as they demonstrate that they are growing up. All children should be encouraged in these areas of responsibility but should be allowed to progress against their individual goals.

A process of learning

Adults should teach skills in self care and helping out with the same patience and recognition that they would approach skills like writing. Children will need to practise and to be encouraged to persevere through the difficult stages. On some tasks they may need the motivation that comes from an adult's friendly push of, 'Come on, I bet you can do it!'

As in any aspect to development, children do not usually learn to do it by themselves all in one go. Adults need to be aware of the progression from the time when adults do a task entirely for children, through the stage of encouraging the children to join in and to the point when an adult is close by but does not intervene unless asked, or to ensure safety.

Children with physical or communication difficulties can still develop self-reliance. Adults must allow them to take some risks and learn from their mistakes. As with the progress of any children, adults have to let go a little in safety.

Personal development, emotions and relationships

This section is slightly different to the others. You will find less information linked to ages and more of a description of the kinds of ways in which children become aware of themselves as individuals and of the wider social world in which they live.

It matters how children feel about themselves. Do they feel confident enough to persevere through difficulties? Are they learning to view themselves as individuals valued by others? Children's feelings about themselves will be intertwined in the unfolding of their development, including their ability to put their feelings and thoughts into words.

What does personal development mean?

Babies and young children become aware of themselves and of the other people in their lives. Of course, you have to be cautious about using words from an adult viewpoint to describe children's feelings. However, babies and children are more alert to the subtleties of what goes on around them than adults often believe.

Consider the following questions as one way of trying to look through a child's eyes. Try to make links between what is described here and the stages of development that are described in other areas of development of the under eights.

'What is me and what is not me?'

Young babies have to discover the physical boundaries between 'me' and 'not me' and 'where do I end and somebody else begins?' By five or six months, the boundaries are clear enough for babies to make some links between 'I do this and then this happens'. For example, babies have learned that a broad smile often brings a smile in return from the adults who care for them. A shout often brings an adult to their side.

'What can I do?'

One and two-year-olds are experimenting with 'can I do this?', 'can I get away with doing this?' and 'can I get someone else to do this for me?' Part of the testing out is also 'have I been forgiven for what I did?'

'Who am I, what makes me "me" ?'

Three, four and five-year-olds develop a growing sense of 'what makes ME'. Their feelings, often strong and perhaps perplexing, become part of a picture of 'me'.

Three and four-year-olds are developing a sense of identity by their personal name and how they belong to a wider community of family and friends.

'What am I like as a person ?'

Children of five, six and seven years reflect at least a little on 'what sort of a person am I?' Children's opinion is formed both by their own feelings and by what other people say directly to them. They start to compare themselves with other children on the measurements they have accepted are important.

'Am I happy with "me"?'

Children as young as five years old have a view of themselves. They have a sense of self-worth, a level of self-esteem in which there is a balance of positives and negatives. Their behaviour, including what they say, will be a reflection of their view.

They have come to conclusions about themselves, that can change over time, as to whether 'I am basically OK'.

Children need a positive sense of self

A positive sense of self and of self-worth is crucial to a child's development. Just as inadequate nutrition can stunt a child's physical growth, so a child whose sense of self includes poor self-esteem or self-dislike may be held back in development. Children will be blocked by a conviction of 'I can't', 'I'm no good', 'I'm different from the others and that's bad'.

Just as food fuels physical growth and well being, so children's experiences and the sense they make of their feelings is the source of their sense of personal identity and how they feel, overall, about themselves.

Children as young as three and four years old may have an overall positive view of themselves or they may feel very negatively. They may feel relatively confident of being able to change, building on their strengths or they may feel hopelessly that what they believe makes them less worthwhile as a person is not something they can change.

Adults responsible for the care and education of the under eights need to consider an overall strategy that actively values all children. A practical aspect to such a strategy has to be that children can see adults to whom they can personally relate – the kind of adult they might be when they grow up.

Hence, children need to see positively reflected in the adult world both sexes, their own ethnic and cultural heritage and some example of disabilities that they are experiencing. A full variety is unlikely to be possible within, say, one staff group, so contact with actual adults has to be supplemented with visits, trips and the full range of play resources and materials.

Children need to see and be able to create themselves in their surroundings – through characters in books, a range of posters, the availability of different paints for accurate skin tones, play materials and equipment, for instance in the home corner, that reflect the diversity of a multicultural society.

Children need adult role models with whom they can positively identify and whom they can see behaving in line with what they say. It is little use women telling girls that they can be electricians if these same women always seek out a man to change a plug. Play resources, as well as the behaviour of known adults, will give messages about not only how the world is but how it might be.

Ethnic and cultural differences

All children need to develop a sense of identity and self-worth, which comes through relating positively to family tradition, culture, ethnic and social group, religion, language and sex. Unless children feel thoroughly secure and free from overpowering worries, then growth in other areas, even their general health can be affected.

It is possible to teach children pride in themselves and their heritage without denigrating or ridiculing other people who are different by ethnic group, religion or sex. Personal confidence does not have to come with a tendency to dismiss others. Unfortunately, some children learn a sense of pride that is intertwined with putting others down through prejudices. An arrogant sense of superiority will prevent young children from any ethnic or religious group from learning about the wider world.

Five and six-year-olds who are aware that their social or cultural group is under-valued may hesitate to express a pride in their identity. Children may even join in unkind so-called jokes against themselves – their ethnicity or a disability – as a form of self-defence. Children of a ethnic or social group that is the butt of prejudice are at high risk of developing a poor self-image. Their families, and other adults who care for them will have to counteract the negative attitudes very actively. Even then, such help can be a serious uphill task, given the prejudices that abound in society.

Children with disabilities

Children's ability to accept their own disability will depend partly on their contact with other disabled children and on watching how adults react to and work with children with a disability.

Children with an impairment, for example, those who need spectacles or a hearing aid, or whose physical skills need the support of a walking frame or a wheelchair can be especially vulnerable to feeling that their differences make them inferior to fully abled children. Much depends on how adults handle the situation and what is said.

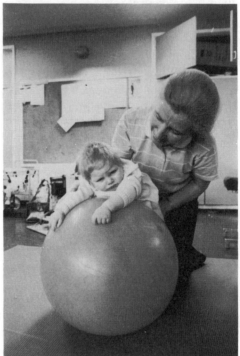

Adrian Rowland

Special attention needs to be paid to children who continue to need assistance in their personal care, for instance in going to the toilet, at an age when their peers are managing without help. These children's dignity and sense of self-worth can be very easily undermined by careless talk and insensitive handling.

Children in a social world

Children grow in awareness of other people around them, both children and adults. They develop relationships and explore the boundaries of friendships. Such development goes hand in hand with their developing capacity to think and reason.

Three and four-year-olds are becoming very aware of what is expected of them, even if such expectations are not built into formal rules. Five to seven-year-olds are learning even more about the kind of behaviour that adults want or will enforce – behaviour that adults might sum up by words like 'cooperative' or 'considerate', or phrases like 'standing up for yourself' or 'healthy competition'.

Children can learn positive attitudes to others through their experiences. They will often move towards one way of behaving rather than another as a result of how adults react. Children are, of course, also influenced by how other children behave and what they say.

For instance, the move to integrate some children with disabilities into nurseries and primary school classes has exposed the children themselves to a broad social environment as well as introducing young children to their peers who may be limited in what they are able to do.

Children with disabilities may react more slowly to events around them or behave in a way more usual for a younger child. Five or six-year-olds can learn to understand the differences in how a friend with disabilities may behave or the kind of help she may appreciate.

Friends will sometimes fall out and argue. Adults could fairly step in if a child's disabilities were used as an insult in an argument. Beyond that, the appropriate approach to an articulate child with physical disabilities would be to let her argue the matter out as a child amongst other children.

Part of understanding children's development is an appreciation that they are increasingly swayed by the opinions and ways of behaving of other children. Adults have to accept and respect such influences, although they can give their reasons for disagreeing with some views. Within reason, adults need to be flexible to the current trends in hair or clothes which influence children as young as seven years.

> As children move into primary school they come under increasing pressure to conform to the behaviour of their peer group. Some of this imitation will be harmless but six and seven-year-olds can be trapped by dares.
>
> In order to help, adults have to show that they recognise - and probably remember – the power of such pressure. Simply saying 'Don't do it' is unlikely to help since children need strategies for getting out of dares.

Learning attitudes

Children develop their sense of self from their day-by-day experience. A major contribution is the reaction of others to them. Such reactions are often shaped by generalised beliefs held about the groups to which children are perceived to belong – their sex, culture or ethnic group. These reactions may be positive, neutral or negative through the hostility of racial prejudice. Strongly held beliefs may lead to the imposition of restrictions, such as 'You're only a girl, so you can't...' or 'Boys don't cry!'

Children initially learn the beliefs held by their family and the associated behaviour that is expected of them. Families may express religious beliefs as well as a moral stance over issues of right and wrong. Some over fives will increasingly question these or the implications for what they have to do or not do. Children will also be swayed by the opinions of their friends and other peers and by what they see in favourite television programmes.

Children are influenced by the society in which they are raised. They are alert to differences between other people, but are dependent on the attitudes expressed by older children and by adults as to how to make sense of these differences.

Children are likely to be aware of ethnic differences but are only learning racial prejudice when such differences are linked to judgements of the superiority of one group over another.

It is a fallacy to claim, as some adults do, that young children are unaware of visible ethnic differences. Especially in an ethnically mixed community, children as young as three years old will be aware of differences in skin colour and other facial features. It would be very surprising if they did not notice, since children are very alert to the world around them.

Awareness of any visible differences does not inevitably lead to prejudice. Yet children can learn prejudiced attitudes as easily as they are learning the vast amount of other information and skills described in the previous areas of development. As stressed throughout this book, children have a great capacity for learning. They will be influenced one way or the other by weight of opinion and the views of adults and children whom they respect. If these attitudes are racist or sexist, then children will repeat such views and copy the behaviour that accompanies them from an early age, certainly younger than five years old.

How might non-racist children behave?

First of all, what shouldn't you be expecting? They certainly won't like every other child they meet. They will have disagreements with other children. They will be rude to each other sometimes. However, children who have been encouraged in a non-racist outlook on life will be much more likely to:

- pick friends on the basis on shared interests and so have friends from different ethnic backgrounds to themselves when this opportunity is available;
- avoid insults based on skin colour or other indicators to ethnic identity;
- allow for different traditions of dress or diet and languages without immediately dubbing these as odd or stupid.

Working positively

Adults can support children by behaving in ways that are described in other parts of the book, especially the explanation of how to encourage children.

Children's emotional development is supported by adults who offer affectionate company as well as help in the more intellectual aspects to development. Adults should respect children's feelings, taking them seriously and never claiming to know better than children themselves how they feel.

Can you remember from your childhood that some adults would actually tell you, 'That doesn't hurt!' when you knew very well that it did, because it was your knee that had been banged or your tooth that was being drilled. How did you feel when that happened or when someone questioned your feelings as well as the physical hurt?

Apparently similar events or experiences will affect children in different ways since they are unique individuals. Children can be happy, excited and content but they can also feel great sadness or emotional hurt.

Sometimes adults convince themselves that children are too young to understand a distressing event such as the death of a parent and that the best way forward is not to talk about the event. Yet children need to grieve as well and cannot cope with a loss if they are not allowed to talk about their feelings. Children are also well aware of disruptions in their lives such as the breakup of a family through divorce. They cannot come to terms with the changes if no one will recognise that they feel confused or angry or sad, or if they are not told what is happening.

Adults may occasionally be surprised by the events that provoke strong feelings from children. It can be helpful to recall from one's own childhood that unfair behaviour from an adult or the hurtful remark of a friend can bite very deep. It is also important to recall that some events, once dealt with, are swiftly shrugged off by children. An adult and a child may have become equally incensed over an argument but the child has often moved on to other events of the day before the adult has stopped being irritated. Adults will help children by dealing with any misbehaviour at the time and resisting any temptation to hark back to it later – the incident is over.

Part of a positive acceptance of children is making sure as an adult that you focus on children's behaviour and help them to keep the ups and downs of everyday life separate from a positive view of themselves. Sometimes children will be told off. Adults may criticise the behaviour, but must leave a child secure in the belief that he or she is liked and accepted as a person.

Children should not be set the unrealistic goal of continuously producing good behaviour – adults certainly do not behave well or considerately all the time. Even three and four-year-olds can feel secure in the belief that, although their misbehaviour has brought down the wrath of adults, this does not make them a bad person. Children reach such a confident belief only if adults behave in line with it - avoiding labels for a child, whether negative or positive – and never using phrases like, 'I won't like you anymore if you....'.

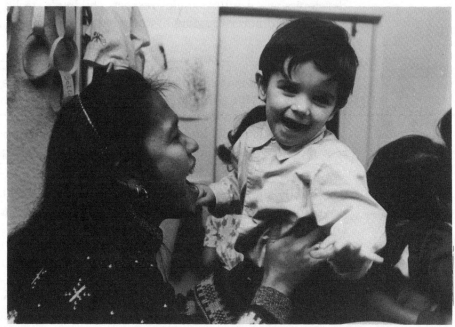

Alison Forbes

Final thoughts

The changes that children go through from birth to eight years are staggering if you view them as a programme of information to learn and skills to be achieved. You should be admiring of children's great ability to learn and their capacity to be interested and thrilled by what they discover. They show great persistence in achieving skills and satisfaction in using the skills they have managed.

Children are sufficiently good at learning that the adult task is to work with this ability and to avoid blocking natural interest and desire to find out by discouraging behaviour or very rigid views of how children should learn or behave. Children show great creative ability and can learn a range of problem solving strategies. Adults can be helpful not only in sharing such strategies but also in supporting children to apply what they have learned to new situations.

Adults have the power to make a major difference to children's lives and their development by what they offer children and by how they behave towards them. They have a responsibility to help children through more difficult phases and support them in dealing with experiences that threaten their development or well being.

Only people who spend very little time with the under eights persist in believing that care and education of this age group is an unskilled or very easy task. Working with or spending time with the under eights is not necessarily all hard work. It can be immensely enjoyable and very satisfying. The skills required do take energy, imagination and patience and, very important, the willingness to understand and continue to learn as an adult about children's development in general and the pattern of individual children.

Further reading

BBC Radio 4 (1999) *Tuning in to children. Understanding a child's development from birth to 5 years*. BBC Educational Developments, and National Children's Bureau. Book and video.

Beaver, M and others (1999) *Babies and young children. Book 1: Early years development*. (2nd ed). London: Stanley Thornes.

Beaver, M and others (1999) *Babies and young children. Book 2: Early years care and education*. (2nd ed). London: Stanley Thornes.

Beaver, M and others (2004) *Babies and young children: NVQ2 early years care and education*. Cheltenham: Nelson Thornes.

Clark, A (2004) *Listening as a way of life. Why and how we listen to young children*. London: National Children's Bureau on behalf of Sure Start.

Clark, A and Moss, P (2001) *Listening to young children: the Mosaic approach*. London: National Children's Bureau.

Council for Disabled Children, Sure Start, and National Children's Bureau (2003) *Early years and the Disability Discrimination Act 1995: what service providers need to know*. London: National Children's Bureau.

Cousins, J (1999) *Listening to four year olds: how they can help us plan their education and care*. London: National Early Years Network.

Cumine, V, Leach, J and Stevenson, G (2000) *Autism in the early years: a practical guide*. London: David Fulton.

Curtis, A and O'Hagan, M (2003) *Care and education in early childhood: a student's guide to theory and practice*. London: RoutledgeFalmer.

Dare, A and O'Donovan, M (2002) *Good practice in caring for young children with special needs*. 2nd ed. Cheltenham: Nelson Thornes.

Dare, A and O'Donovan, M (2003) *A practical guide to working with babies*. 3rd ed. Cheltenham: Nelson Thornes.

David, T and others (2003) *Birth to three matters: a review of the literature compiled to inform The Framework to Support Children in Their Earliest Years*. London: Department for Education and Skills. (Research report; no. 444).

Deudney, C (2002) *Play and autism*. London: National Autistic Society. (National Autistic Society Factsheet).

Devereux, J (2003) *Working with children in the early years*. London: David Fulton.

Dickins, M (2004) *Listening as a way of life. Listening to young disabled children*. London: National Children's Bureau on behalf of Sure Start.

Dickins, M and Denziloe, J (2003) *All together: how to create inclusive services for disabled children and their families*. 2nd ed. London: National Children's Bureau.

Early Childhood Education Forum (2003) *Quality in diversity in early learning: a framework for early childhood practitioners*. Rev ed. London: National Children's Bureau.

Early Childhood Education Forum (2003) *Key times for play*. Maidenhead: Open University.

Edwards, AG (2002) *Relationships and learning: caring for children from birth to three*. London: National Children's Bureau.

Gerhardt, S (2004) *Why love matters: how affection shapes a baby's brain*. Hove: Brunner-Routledge.

Goldschmied, E (1986) *Infants at work: babies of 6-9 months exploring everyday objects*. London: National Children's Bureau. Video.

Goldschmied, E and Hughes, A (1992) *Heuristic play with objects: children of 12-20 months exploring everyday objects*. National Children's Bureau. Video.

Jackson, S (2004) *People under three: young children in day care*. 2nd ed. London: Routledge.

Lindon, J (2003) *Child care and early education: good practice to support young children and their families*. London: Thomson.

Lindon, J (2000) *Helping babies and toddlers learn: a guide to good practice with under-threes*. London: National Early Years Network.

Lindon, J, Kelman, K, and Sharp, A (2001) *Play and learning for the under 3's*. London: TSL Education.

Lindon, J (1998) *Understanding child development: knowledge, theory and practice*. London: Macmillan.

McLarnon, J (2004) *Listening as a way of life. Supporting parents and carers to listen: a guide for practitioners*. London: National Children's Bureau on behalf of Sure Start.

Mortimer, H (2001) *Personal, social and emotional development of children in the early years*. Lichfield: QEd.

Mortimer, H (2003) *Trackers 0-3*. Lichfield: QEd.

Mortimer, H (2004) *Trackers 3-5*. Lichfield: QEd.

Newman, S (2004) *Stepping out: using games and activities to help your child with special needs*. London: Jessica Kingsley.

Paley, VG (2001) *In Mrs Tulley's room: a childcare portrait*. London: Harvard University Press.

Rich, D (2004) *Listening as a way of life. Listening to babies*. London: National Children's Bureau on behalf of Sure Start.

Robinson, A (2004) *Working with young children from minority ethnic groups: a guide to sources of information*. London: Early Childhood Unit, National Children's Bureau for the Sure Start Unit.

Robinson, A (2004) *Working with young children who have special needs or disabilities: a guide to sources of information*. London: Early Childhood Unit, National Children's Bureau for the Sure Start Unit. Downloadable from: www.surestart.gov.uk

Robinson, M (2003) *From birth to one: the year of opportunity*. Buckingham: Open University.

Wolfendale, S (1998) *All about me*. 2nd ed. Nottingham: NES/Arnold.

Index

Growing up

From eight years to young adulthood

Jennie Lindon

Published by National Children's Bureau Enterprises Ltd. February 1996. 200pp. ISBN 1 874579 61 X

The sequel to the best-selling ***Child Development from Birth to Eight***, ***Growing Up*** describes the main changes for children and young people as they grow from middle childhood to the brink of adulthood. A full description of development is placed in the context of their daily lives and those of their families.

The book explores the meaning of independence for a generation that is growing up in a world that is different from that of their parents' childhood. Yet many of the concerns of today's children and young people are scarcely different from those of previous generations: the experience of school, making friends and dealing with the pressures and risks of growing up. The book includes the views of children and young people themselves, as well as those of adults reflecting on their own youth.

Growing Up offers new perspectives and practical suggestions to adults who are concerned with older children and young people. Parents will find it useful for understanding their own sons and daughters. The book will be equally valuable to teachers, youth workers, play workers, professionals within the police or the probation services, social workers, nurses in adolescent units and workers in residential homes.

'a useful route map to a child's journey through the jungle of adolescence' (*The Guardian*)

Price: £11.00 Bureau members, £14.00 non-members

To order, contact Book Sales, National Children's Bureau, 8 Wakley Street, London EC1V 7QE. Telephone: 0171 843 6028/9; Fax 0171 278 9512

For further information about National Children's Bureau publications, or to receive our current catalogue, contact Book Sales.

Membership

Members of the National Children's Bureau receive discounts on publications as well as access to our Library and Information service and a wide range of other benefits. To find out more about membership, contact the Membership Office on 0171 843 6047.